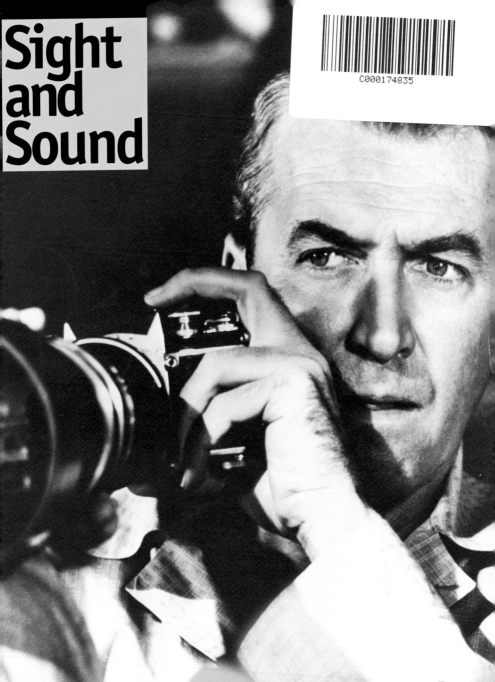

Sight and Sound

C000174835

Get a close-up on the real film action
Subscribe now – save 33%

BIG GRANNY AND LITTLE EDEN

'Gallivant' is a new kind of British film, a breathless dash around the nation's coasts that outwits the industry, argues Iain Sinclair

FROM THE TOP OF THE HILL

Ravishing and story-driven, 'Gabbeh' is banned in its native Iran. Mohsen Makhmalbaf, its director, talks about movies and stories to Hodaei Ditmars

British...

International...

COMPULSION

Was Hitchcock a closet Surrealist? With the re-release of 'Vertigo' in 70mm, Peter Wollen examines mystery, perversion and psychosis in the most personal of the director's films

KISS KISS BANG BANG

In his new, extravagant version of 'Romeo & Juliet', Baz Luhrmann makes the story a visceral epic. He exploits camp, cars and guns to turn Shakespeare into cinema — and his words into real movie dialogue. By José Arroyo

Classic...

Passionate...

Why make a homage to 50s Monster Culture in the 90s? J. Hoberman on 'Mars Attacks!'

PAX AMERICANA

ALI'S RUMBLE

Provocative...

Unique

CHATHAM GRAMMAR SCHOOL
FOR GIRLS

INDEX
ON CENSORSHIP

NOT TO BE
TAKEN AWAY

INDEX ON CENSORSHIP 6 1997

WEBSITE NEWS UPDATED EVERY TWO WEEKS

www.oneworld.org/index_oc/
indexoncenso@gn.apc.org
tel: 0171-278 2313
fax: 0171-278 1878

Volume 26 No 6 November/December 1997 Issue 179

Index on Censorship (ISSN 0306-4220) is published bi-monthly by a non-profit-making company: Writers & Scholars International Ltd, Lancaster House, 33 Islington High Street, London N1 9LH. *Index on Censorship* is associated with Writers & Scholars Educational Trust, registered charity number 325003
Periodicals postage: (US subscribers only) paid at Newark, New Jersey. Postmaster: send US address changes to *Index on Censorship* c/o Mercury Airfreight Int/ Ltd Inc, 2323 Randolph Avenue, Avenel, NJ 07001, USA
© This selection Writers & Scholars International Ltd, London 1997
© Contributors to this issue, except where otherwise indicated

Subscriptions (6 issues per annum)
Individuals: UK £38, US $50, rest of world £43
Institutions: UK £42, US $72, rest of world £48
Students: UK £25, US $35, rest of world £31
Speak to Syra on 0171 278 2313

Former Editors: Michael Scammell (1972-81); Hugh Lunghi (1981-83); George Theiner (1983-88); Sally Laird (1988-89); Andrew Graham-Yooll (1989-93)

EDITORIAL

Privacy at what price?

THE European Convention on Human Rights has been an effective instrument for protecting both privacy and free expression as equal human rights. Its incorporation into British law is a milestone which will have a profound effect on British political culture. But on privacy itself, unresolved questions remain: the Convention, with its broad, abstract principles, will allow judges to establish the law on a case-by-case basis, with clear public interest defence or other safeguards needed by the media not necessarily taken into account. Some have argued that the media might prefer a privacy law laid down in statute, addressing its particular concerns.

Here Arthur Davidson opposes this and suggests tougher self-regulation with financial penalties. Others propose a limited law of privacy in return for reform of the libel laws and the promised Freedom of Information Act. This may seem a good trade off, but there are dangers, given the myriad laws which already act as constraints on journalists (p36). Abuse of press power is unacceptable, but a free press is the still the most effective instrument for holding the powerful to account and breaking taboos. And it's alarming that, in democratic Britain, *Private Eye* was banned from two large retail chains after exposing the more hypocritical stances of the media and the public over Diana's death.

And *where* should privacy be respected? Geoffrey Robertson says generally in the cradle, the school, the bed, the hospital and the grave. 'For the photographer', says Philip Griffith Jones, a distinguished photo-journalist, 'anything seen in public can be recorded.' And what about those places which can only flourish and fester behind a wall of secrecy, where we *need* the camera to intrude where authority does not want it? We publish a photographer's story from Algeria's terrible war and the first photographs from the women's wing of Evin, Iran's most infamous and closely guarded prison. The answer must be to treat privacy and free expression as *complementary* human rights.

But the brouhaha over press intrusion has obscured the fact that, for most people in the developed world, technology in the hands of big business and government makes far greater inroads into their privacy. According to Simon Davies, every adult is located on average in 200 computer databases. (p44) Next year the European Data Protection directive will place some controls on electronic surveillance, data analysis and the use of sensitive personal information. If ordinary people's private lives are really to be protected, these measures too will have to bite. ❏

contents

New York wall mural – Credit: Nevine Mabro

R.I.P
1961-1997

'No one should forget that there exists a direct relationship between each cubic metre of flowers placed before the palace and every square metre of photographs printed of the princess.'

A photographer's tale – p26

LETTERS

Restoring the balance

From Julia Hall
Northern Ireland Researcher
Human Rights Watch, NYC

In his critique of Human Rights Watch's 1997 report on police abuse in Northern Ireland, *To Serve Without Favour: Policing Human Rights, and Accountability in Northern Ireland* (Index 4/1997), Sir Louis Blom-Cooper categorically claims that there is *no* physical ill-treatment of detainees in Northern Ireland's notorious holding centres. As for psychological abuse, Blom-Cooper asserts that the 'self discipline' of supposed terrorists provides them with a coping mechanism for the 'austere conditions' of short-term detention.

These extraordinary and spurious claims are premised on a series of annual reports written by Blom-Cooper himself in his capacity as the UK government-appointed 'independent' commissioner for the four holding centres. They are based on his personal observations of interrogation sessions over the last four years. According to Blom-Cooper's 1996 report, however, he and his deputy have observed '*something less than one half of one percent*' of all interrogations conducted since 1992. The UN Human Rights Committee, UN Committee Against Torture, European Committee for the Prevention of Torture, Amnesty International, and Human Rights Watch somehow got access to some of the remaining 99 per cent of those interrogated who consistently and credibly claim that such abuses regularly occur. Moreover, in the same 1996 report, Blom-Cooper himself expresses concern about persistent allegations of verbal abuse, intimidation and harassment by RUC detectives during interrogation, and calls for audio and video-taping of all interrogations, preventive measures yet to be implemented by the UK government.

Blom-Cooper's assertion that allegations of harassment and intimidation of Northern Ireland's defence lawyers are 'oft repeated, but unsubstantiated' is also without foundation. Human Rights Watch has interviewed numerous defence lawyers, including Protestant representatives of the Law Society of Northern Ireland, who claim that such intimidation is routine. Catholic defence lawyer Patrick Fincane was harassed and threatened with death by RUC detectives interrogating his clients in holding centres. In 1989, Fincane was murdered by loyalist paramilitaries at his home in front of his wife and three children. Persistent allegations of lawyer harassment and serious irregularities in the investigation into Patrick Fincane's killing have convinced the UN Special Rapporteur on the Independence of Judges and Lawyers to conduct a fact-finding mission to the UK and Northern Ireland in September-October 1997. Significantly, the Special Rapporteur's areas of special concern this year are the UK (particularly Northern Ireland) and Turkey.

With respect to our investigation of the policing of contentious parades and marches, Blom-Cooper's own credibility would be enhanced if he had actually read the report. Sir Louis accuses us of being 'selective' by allegedly failing to mention the government-established Independent Review of Parades and Marches chaired by Dr Peter North and tasked with evaluating the then current arrangements for handling public processions in Northern Ireland. We direct Blom-Cooper's attention to the section of our report entitled 'Independent Review of Parades and Marches' which details the composition, methodology and recommendations of the North Commission.

Blom-Cooper's sympathy for the RUC Chief Constable's 'frustration at being caught in the middle' of disputes arising from the marching season predictably ignores the RUC's contribution to the tensions and violence that resulted in the collapse of the rule of law that characterised the 1996 (and July 1997) marching season. Under the guise of ensuring 'public safety' the RUC has cleared the way for contentious Orange marches by physically assaulting peaceful nationalist protesters, using sectarian language in the

course of police operations, indiscriminately firing thousands of potentially lethal plastic bullets and sealing off entire communities for lengthy periods of time, denying people access to their children, elderly or infirm relatives, shops, medical care and the right to protest. Both the UK government-appointed Northern Ireland Standing Advisory Commission on Human Rights (SACHR) and the US State Department's *Country Reports on Human Rights Practices for 1996* state that the decisions and actions taken by the RUC during the 1996 marching season severely damaged the RUC's reputation as an impartial force.

Human Rights Watch challenges Blom-Cooper to take his own advice – to write about the facts objectively, not from the biased and self-preserving role of government apologist that he has so eagerly embraced. ❏

Blaming the victim

From Ike Okonta
London Office of Environmental Rights Action, Nigeria

John Jennings, former chairman of Shell UK claims (Index 4/1997) that Shell does not interfere in the political affairs of Nigeria. This has not been our experience in the Niger Delta. Officials of Shell Nigeria work closely with the Nigerian military *junta* to suppress and brutalise the local communities whenever they complain about the devastation of their environment by the company's oil exploration and production activities.

In September 1990, the people of Umuechem, a Niger Delta community, adopted peaceful means to protest the pollution of their farmlands by Shell. Shell officials invited government anti-riot police to 'deal' with the protesters. Ninety villagers lay dead by the time the heavily armed policemen had restored 'peace' to the community. In an interview with *Sunday Times* journalists in December 1995, Colonel Paul Okuntimo, former commander of a military task force set up by the government to suppress the Ogoni and the other oil communities, revealed that the oil company provided him with money and logistical support. A team of Human Rights Watch/Africa officials who visited the Niger Delta a few months previously had established that Okuntimo and the soldiers in his command were responsible for mass murder, torture, the sacking of several towns and villages and the rape of women and little girls in communities that were involved in the protest against Shell's despoliation of their environment.

Ken Saro-Wiwa, leader of the Movement for the Survival of the Ogoni People (MOSOP) who was murdered by the Nigerian *junta* in November 1995, was not 'fighting an internal political battle'. Saro-Wiwa was a writer and environmental activist who was concerned that 35 years of Shell's oil production in Ogoniland had brought the community nothing but poverty, misery and the destruction of their farmlands and fishing ponds through massive oil spillage and indiscriminate gas flaring. MOSOP and Saro-Wiwa petitioned Shell in 1992 to put an end to this odious practice and pay adequate compensation to the victims of environmental pollution. Shell officials refused and called in Nigerian troops instead. The murder of 2,000 Ogoni people, including Saro-Wiwa, and the uproar it generated worldwide in the media, was the consequence.

Shell has found it convenient to blame the local communities for oil spills in their areas, accusing them of deliberately sabotaging pipelines in order to claim compensation from the company, but has not been able to back up this claim with concrete evidence. In July 1996, the British Advertising Standards Authority ruled that Shell's claim that 'over 60 per cent of spills were caused by sabotage' was not substantiated and warned the company to stop peddling this falsehood. Demonise and criminalise the local communities, then call in the dogs of war: this has been Shell's well-known strategy in the Niger Delta since it struck oil in the area in 1956. ❏

● **'We aim to put the FUN back in fundamentalism'** goes the slogan. Following the Vatican's lead, Islamist organisations such as Hamas, Hezbollah and Islamic Gateway - they of the above rubric - have established Web sites in which 'Comfort Zones' offer, among other things, dating and marriage services for Muslims and religious advice on the joys of polygamy. Try www.academic.marist.edu or http:ummah.org.uk

● *Moscow News,* a journal with no love for President Alaksander Lukashenka of neighbouring Belarus, has reported yet one more of his unfortunate - and repeated - malapropisms. 'From now on,' the president told a press conference, 'official sources of information will only be accessible to journalists who have been discredited.' Plenty of them around, apparently.

● **Chelyabinsk, the heartland** of the Russian military nuclear industry and a 'closed' city in Soviet times, is still not a safe place for advocates of openness in environmental matters. Physicist Nikolay Schur and his wife, watchdogs on radioactive and other contamination issues in the region, currently face prosecution for embezzling their own money.

● **The UK book shop chain,** W H Smith, says it will not stock the forthcoming novel *The End of Alice* by A M Holmes, after the

National Society for the Prevention of Cruelty to Children asked retailers not to stock it on the grounds that reading it could incite paedophiles to commit offences against children.

● **The dogs bark and the caravan...**Disney are facing calls for boycotts by Arab and Catholic groups based on the unfair representations of ethnic and professional groups in their productions because they reproduce stereotypes. The American-Arab Anti-Discrimination Committee accuses Disney of launching 'a holy war against Arabs'. The focus of its ire is the film *GI Jane* which, they say, 'features a gratuitous end sequence with star Demi Moore and her Navy Seal chums on a rampage killing Arabs'.

● **The Catholic League**, meanwhile, is petitioning Disney chairman Michael Eisner to withdraw *Nothing Sacred* because it lives up to its promise and portrays priests who question the existence of God.

● **And in the UK**, the National Federation of the Blind tried to ban the Disney cartoon *Mr Magoo* for its negative portrayal of the blind. Their American counterparts, however, have accepted a pay-off, with part of the royalties to be donated to charities for the blind.

● **World-renowned graphic designer** Milton Glaser, who designed the 'I love New York' logo and co-founded *New York* magazine, has repudiated his nomination for the coveted Chrysler Award for Innovation in Design. The decision followed his discovery that, since January 1996, Chrysler's advertising agency has demanded pre-publication approval of editorial content in magazines which carry its ads. The influence of advertising on editorial is a hot issue in the US. Glaser told readers of the *Nation* how a friend had once taken a copy of *Vogue* and attached a coloured thread to every ad that related to some editorial mention in the issue. 'The results,' he wrote, 'looked like a small Persian rug'.

● **A Californian resident** refused on 22 August to return *The New Joy of Gay Sex* to her San Mateo county library and intends to store the book in a locker because it 'doesn't meet the standards set forth by society'. Less than a week later councilwoman Gloria Sankuer was facing discipline in Warren City after a librarian refused to show her how to access pornographic images on a public terminal. 'My need was urgent,' she explained. 'I needed pictures of this disgusting, appalling porno on the Internet.' She added that the librarian should, in her case, have made an exception to the rule banning libraries from accessing pornography, since she was a member of a country commission looking into web pornography.

● **The art of the nude** received a different kind of setback on 21 October when police ordered two dimly-recognisable 'pixellated' paintings of male and female bodies to be removed from the window of London's Colville Place Gallery. The two paintings by German artist Rolf Gnewuch formed part of the exhibition 'The Sacred Pixel - Art, Sex and Censorship'. Police insisted the gallery display a warning that some of the work might be considered offensive. 'Since we displayed the offensive material notice,' said gallery-owner Keith Watson, 'practically all the visitors we have had tend to be extremely odd.'

● **'Censorship is censorship,'** said Jeremy Irons at the Venice film Festival in early September, following a preview of the film *Chinese Box*, by Hong Kong director Wayne Wang, in which the British actor plays a journalist. But he was not referring to China, where the authorities hold the negatives of a film until it is approved, but to the US, where the distribution of Irons' recent movie, a re-make of Vladimir Nabokov's *Lolita* is held up by a major Hollywood studio on grounds of taste. The Venice festival also saw the first showing of *Keep Cool,* by Zhang Yimou, director of *Red Sorghum* and *To Live.* Beijing reportedly blocked its showing at the Cannes festival in May because it portrayed a backward China.

● **In vino non veritas** goes the saying in Moscow. The influx of western advertising slogans that have flooded Russia since the collapse of the Empire is worrying Russian scholars concerned for the purity of the language. Measures to restrict their use have had only limited success: the new *nomenklatura* — the *biznesmeny* — still seek western *no-khau*, dress their children in *dzinzy* and buy them *gamburgery* and *kola*. More draconian purges of the language are threatened but, for now, we have it on the highest authority, namely Serghey Prikhodko, foreign policy aide to President Boris Yeltsin, that 'champagne' and 'cognac' will not be among the banned words. Reports that the matter was discussed over dinner during the recent visit of President Jacques Chirac had 'nothing to do with reality', according to Prikhodko. He said that 'neither champagne, cognac nor vodka came up for discussion' and supposed the speculation in the media must have resulted from 'over-indulgence in the beverages concerned'. *Vera Rich*

● **Even crocodiles get the blues** Anyone expecting a carnival in Kinshasa after the death of ousted dictator, Mobutu Sese Seko would have been surprised by the sheer bittersweetness, as news filtered into the capital of his former plantation-empire in the early hours of 8 September. State-controlled Radio-Télévision Nationale Congolaise failed to carry the story on its first morning bulletin but, by 7am, news of Mobutu's death had spread through the bouganvillias and *bidonvilles*. Not surprisingly, it wiped Princess Diana's funeral from the front-page of all 20 or so independent newspapers in Kinshasa. But the headlines were neither virulent, nor caustic. 'No tears for Mobutu?' read the headline in *La Reference Plus*, which quoted a former ambassador to Paris saying that Mobutu must have regretted not asking his people for their forgiveness. A historian, cited in the same pages, described him as 'a case apart, unique among other dictators'. The pro-Mobutu *Le Soft* boomed: 'History closes around a man,' going on to examine the leopard-man's legacy. His rule, the paper commented, was one of 'theft and anarchy ...but he fashioned a nation, which is now threatened by a foreign occupation alliance', a reference to the Rwandan and Ugandan soldiers who play a crucial role in maintaining the regime of President Laurent Kabila in the re-named Democratic Republic of Congo. *Penny Dale*

● **Colombian carry on** By the eve of municipal elections on 26 October, Colombia's two leading rebel groups, the Revolutionary Armed Forces of Colombia (FARC) and the National Liberation Army (ELN) had successfully kept their promise to disrupt the elections, weaken the national government and bring the country to a standstill. While President Ernesto Samper desperately tried to maintain some semblance of law and order, Colombians faced a situation where there could well have been no names on the ballot papers when they arrived to vote. In the last couple of months, 30 candidates have been assassinated, over 200 kidnapped and 1,900 have withdrawn fearing for their lives. 'I choose life,' said one candidate, as he pulled out of the race.

Samper, determined not to lose face nationally or internationally, increased the powers of the military after a 'council of war' meeting with army generals; 50

international observers were imported to ensure the integrity of the mayoral races. Not to be outdone, on 23 October, ELN rebels promptly seized two of the observers, Raul Martinez of Chile and Manfredo Marroquin of Guatemala, in a provocative move aimed at humiliating the government.

Both the left-wing rebels and the right-wing paramilitary groups banned campaigning in their rural strongholds and put forward their own candidates, thinly disguised as independents, in an attempt to seize power. The outcome of Sunday's elections is irrelevant: democracy has been sidelined and the real contest to determine who controls Colombia, lies ahead. *Nevine Mabro*

● **The icing of Danny Hernandez** Manila Press Club has always had a policy requiring visitors to check their weapons at the door. But only recently has there been a need to enforce it. Pistols have become essential accessories for the city's media fraternity, since the killing of the tabloid journalist Danny Hernandez three months ago. Talk at the club bar these days is about calibres, magazine capacity and rates of fire. 'I know that a lot of the reporters now carry guns,' said Joven Custodio, associate editor of the *People's Tonight* newspaper.

People's Tonight staff are particularly concerned since it was their star columnist, Danny Hernandez, who died in what is seen as the worst attack on the Philippine media since the Marcos dictatorship ended over a decade ago. The murder was the first of a journalist in Manila in living memory. His body was found on the back seat of a taxi in a suburban street in the early hours of 3 June. He had been shot in the head minutes after leaving his office. The Philippines' press is regarded as one of the freest in Asia and it played a central role in the downfall of the Marcos regime. But Hernandez's death has severely dented its confidence.

Hernandez's killer was most likely one of the country's drug lords, who have created a major social problem with crystal amphetamine or 'ice'. An estimated three million Filipinos are addicted, generating huge profits for traffickers who import the raw material from China for refining.

Dealers were a regular target of Danny Hernandez's column. At the time of his death, he had had been working on an enquiry into links between traffickers, police and politicians. Among the names he revealed was Florencio Parena, a senior police officer who went into hiding soon after the killing. Eventually captured in a police raid, Parena denied involvement in the murder, but implicated Alfredo Tiongco, a Chinese-Filipino wanted for drug offences who had also been accused by Hernandez. Parena claimed that he and Tiongco had enjoyed the protection of a prominent politician and former screen comic, Senator Vicente Soto. Soto is now under investigation. Hernandez began receiving death threats a few months earlier, according to a photographer colleague. 'Then one day a package arrived for him. Inside the box was a new *polo barong* (the traditional Filipino long shirt, used to dress bodies for burial) and two 45 calibre bullets. That message was clear enough.' *Barry Lowe*

JUDITH VIDAL–HALL

The killing spree

Behind the recent massacres in Algeria lies a darker struggle: war between the rival clans of the military government, one now in a marriage of convenience with the armed wing of the banned Islamic Salvation Front, the other fighting to ensure its for survival behind a democratic facade

THE Algerian municipal elections of 23 October took place in the shadow of a killing spree unprecedented in the five years of a brutal civil war. At least 150,000 have died in Algeria since 1992, but massacres of this kind – up to 200 and 300 at a time – have not been seen since the army ruthlessly and systematically exterminated families thought to be connected to the Islamic Salvation Front (FIS) and its armed wing, the Islamic Salvation Army (AIS) in 1993-1995.

Since July this year, over 1,500 people, many of them women, babies and small children, have lost their lives in a series of mass murders in villages of the Mitidja around Algiers. Many have been in garrison towns within shouting distance of army barracks. Many have lasted hours while the army stood by, arriving on the scene only when the job was done and the perpetrators fled. How to explain the reluctance of the military to intervene? That the attacks are in an area that voted massively for FIS in the 1991 elections, aborted after the Islamists looked set to win in the final round of voting?

Many explanations for the summer's orgy of killing have been put forward: the coming of elections and the anxiety of government and army to eradicate opposition; the dying throes of the Islamic Armed Groups (GIA), now divided internally, poorly equipped and, since the Armed Islamic Group's (AIS) ceasefire and truce with the regular army, on the run from the combined forces attacking them in their strongholds in the Mitidja; and the renewed infighting between rival clans in the military establishment divided between 'eradicators' and 'conciliators'. The (FIS) is also in some disarray.

Weakened by the army's war on it since it was robbed of victory in the aborted parliamentary elections of December 1991 and subsequently banned, its leadership appears divided on the deal between its own armed wing, the AIS, and the army. 'FIS was the first to call for a ceasefire,' says the acting leader of FIS, 'but the authorities preferred to deal with our military wing, the AIS. They have always chosen to treat this crisis as a security matter rather look for a political solution.'

Rumours of coups are probably far-fetched: the army has nothing to gain. Government is entirely under its thumb. The military were the king-makers of the present regime from among its ranks; President General Liamine Zeroual, endorsed by the USA and France, was their man. Meanwhile, like so many armies before them, Algeria's generals are milking the economy for all it's worth. The recovery of the dollar and the rise in oil prices – plus good rains this year – have given a spurious boost to the economy that has nothing to do with good management or an increase in productivity.

While the army fills its pockets and the country burns, nothing of the unprecedented US$8 billion in foreign reserves nor the US$6 billion balance of payments surplus for the first quarter of 1997 trickles down to the population. For the first time since independence, unemployment, officially, stands at 30 per cent; inflation is up to 112 per cent; industrial production is down eight per cent; the middle class are pauperised; illnesses that had disappeared have returned as a result of malnutrition, the collapse of public health systems and the absence of even basic drugs. Those that are available, all imported, sell on the black market for prohibitive prices. As a candidate for Hamas – a legal Islamic party now with seats in government – pointed out to the *Independent*'s Robert Fisk during his election visit to Algeria, 'this, too, is a form of terrorism'.

Censorship of the local press and the exclusion of the foreign press corps has ensured that the real story of Algeria's war has gone largely untold. When it has been, it has been in terms of militant Islamic fundamentalism fighting against brave attempts to bring democracy to a country that has spent the years since independence in the grip of aging and corrupt one-party rule. Much what the government would have the world and its own citizens believe. As we have tried to show in *Index* since 1994, the reality is more obscure, more complex – less newsworthy.

Since 1994, *Index* has followed the course of a dirty war in which friend and foe have the same face, both shrouded in the secrecy of state censorship behind which government and armed groups alike terrorise a population and intimidate a press into silence. We have given silenced voices a hearing: the Algerian independent press, as well as the voices of reconciliation within FIS, have found a platform. The excesses of the Algerian armed forces as well as those of the terrorists within the Groupe Islamique Armé (GIA) were held to account before it was the fashion. The courage of journalists like Salima Ghezali of the French-language Algerian daily *Nation*, has been honoured; the sham democracy behind which the army hides its grip on the country, exposed.

With the 23 October elections, the foreign press corps was allowed in to see for themselves the government's crowning achievement: what a spokesmen called 'the last stone in the edifice of our democracy'. It came as no surprise that the ruling National Rally for Democracy, the party recently reconstituted by President Liamine Zeroual from among the bickering and corrupt Front de Libération National (FLN) that had ruled Algeria since independence, claimed a healthy turn out – over 66 per cent – and a resounding majority of 55 per cent. FIS could not stand; other parties, around 30 in all, did. Two at least among them, the moderate Islamic party Hamas, currently with seats in government, and the largely Berber and secular Rally for Culture and Democracy (RCD), are claiming massive fraud.

Despite claims by the government that 'everything went off normally', there was a massive police and army presence at polling stations and in the main towns. Turnout was slow and not much above 20 per cent in some areas; the recent spate of massacres in towns and villages around the capital is still too recent for anyone to suppose that these elections will end the violence – or put food on their plates.

The army is diverted to spend more time guarding the pipelines in the south than protecting a civilian population at the mercy of the exactions of Islamist and security forces alike; and for the squabbling generals, it's business as usual. ❏

Judith Vidal-Hall

MICHEL GUERRIN

Algerian icon

It took a single photograph to alert the world's media to the nightmare that is Algeria. Taken by a local news photographer after a massacre in which over 200, many women and small children among them, died, it was distributed by AFP and made the front pages of the press throughout Europe and the USA

THIS is a picture of a mother on her knees supported by another mother. It is, in short, a Pietà: an image we observe carrying a wealth of our own cultural baggage. The Madonna in Hell. One more massacre in Algeria, this time in Bentalha, a village a few kilometres from Algiers. The icon is timeless, not a news pic: but then news has little meaning in Algeria today.

Stripped of everything else, this photo is about grief; grief so intense we can see, in our mind's eye, the rows of corpses lined up in the early hours of the morning. Its use on the front pages of most French, Spanish, Italian and Lebanese dailies, plus the *Herald Tribune*, the *Washington Post* and the *Los Angeles Times* contributed to the creation of an image that was about to become the icon of the Algerian war.

It carries a weight of emotion – and some information: 'The woman below has just lost all eight of her children; the women supporting her has just lost her parents'. All murdered in Beltalha. The photographer, Hocine, is Agence France Presse's (AFP) only accredited photographer in Algeria. Why, he muses, was it that particular shot of the three he took that day, that caught the imagination of the media? On 29 August, just after the massacre in Raïs, he got a similar shot of a woman, her face transfigured by grief, miming the scene of throat slitting with her hands. It was an extraordinary shot but made scarcely any impact.

The story of photojournalism bristles with such 'Pietàs': women weeping over the fallen on fields of battle, for instance. They are more 'acceptable' than pictures of the butchery itself or of pregnant women eviscerated. 'Humankind cannot bear too much blood,' says Goskin Sipahioglu, head of the photo agency Sipa. So, they're offered a palliative image that arouses their pity.

In Algeria, the picture did not appear in any of the country's 10 independent dailies. They have their own photographers,but they didn't get this shot.

Events the day after the massacre at Bentalha on 22 September illustrate the difficulties of being a photographer in a country where, according to a local press photographer, 'A camera is considered more dangerous than a Kalashnikov. People are far more accustomed to seeing weapons than cameras.'

Alerted to the massacre, a few photographers reached the site around 9.00AM. 'Everything was extremely confused,' says Hocine. 'Buildings were charred and there was the smell of burning. I was stopped by police in plain clothes four or five times; I couldn't get my camera out. The bodies of the victims had been laid out in a school; there was no way of getting in without running the gauntlet of the people hanging around outside.' Another Algerian photographer claimed he was manhandled, insulted and had his film confiscated.

In an attempt to find out exactly how many had been massacred, a reporter

'Just one more massacre': the photo that shook the world – Credit: Hocine/AFP

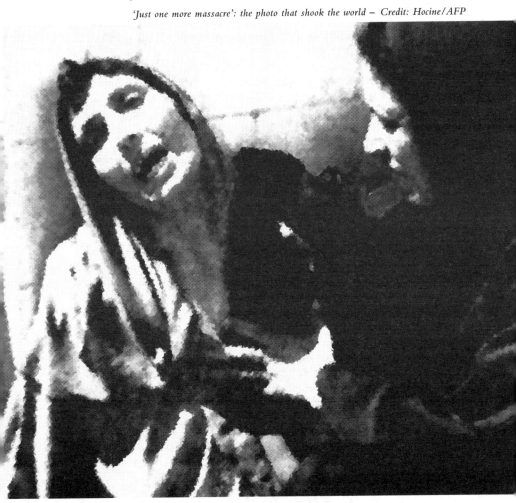

from *Al Watan* managed to get into the cemetery. 'It's standard practice: we counted the graves. The official figure was 85 dead; we made it 252.' Be that as it may, most photographers question themselves on the significance of their pictures. 'The massacres happen at night. By the time we get there, the blood is still fresh on the walls,' one of them explains. 'We can see where the terrorists have stamped in the blood and spread it around, or smeared their hands with it to leave their imprints on the walls. But short of having a friend in security or the fire brigade, there's no way we can get to see the victims.'

Getting the news out has got even more difficult since the massacre at Raïs on 29 August. While there is no formal ban, getting a picture is purely a matter of luck: what time the photographer gets there, the mood of the police, what sort of deal can be cut by negotiating. 'It's a game of hide and seek,' says one photographer who uses a tiny 'spy camera' to worm his way in. Even for him, he says, things have got 'much tougher'. Which is why Hocine goes for pictures that probe beyond the surface; 'more about emotions than news'. This emotion is to be found not so much at the actual sites of the massacres, which are 'too well guarded', but on 'the faces of survivors'.

HOCINE's famous photograph was not, therefore, taken in the village – as many reports have said – but at Al Harrach hospital on the outskirts of Algiers where about a hundred or so people, mainly mothers, had gathered in the hope of discovering survivors. They were not allowed inside the hospital, but searched through the lists of names pinned up at the entrance.

After discovering there was no hope for any of her eight children, the woman in his photo crumpled to the ground, almost fainting. Hocine leaned over and snapped while the police were otherwise occupied. As a precaution, he removed the film and jumbled it with others in his bag. Moments later, the new film was indeed stripped out of his camera by the police – but the one that mattered survived. At 3.22pm the same day, the film was being distributed worldwide via the AFP network.

Hocine is one of around 20 press photographers – some say far fewer – who work for Algerian dailies, usually in black and white. Most of his somewhat older generation have given up the unequal struggle and no longer work; the risks are too great. Faced with the additional problem of visas and insurance, there are few foreign photographers on the scene either.

The job of gathering the evidence of a country at war is left to a younger generation of Algerian photographers, 'most of them well under 25-years-old' according one reporter. They have no experience nor training yet they have 'a burning desire to break new ground', to leave nothing untouched. When their work was exhibited at the Festival of Photojournalism in Perpignan, its director commented on the 'freshness' of their work, 'their preoccupation with bearing witness rather than with artistic form'.

When the police accuse us of being 'enemies of Algeria', 'traitors', 'sold out', 'swine', 'bastards who are giving a false impression of the country', we have to have thick skins. 'You also have to pad yourself out to hide your kit from prying eyes in crowded streets when going around town,' says an editor. One photographer says he's not slept in his own bed for five years: 'Sure I'm afraid. But this is what I've chosen to do to get the news.' These are the 'solitaries' who often work anonymously and no longer credit their pictures for security reasons.

A number of editors and photographers have noticed a change in the role of pictures in the daily press. 'Photography is more and more important; words no longer want to speak,' says a journalist with *Al Watan*. 'When words have lost the power to convey the horror of this endless succession of unspeakable atrocities, photos take over and fill out the front page.'

More humdrum pictures of everyday life or the relationship between people and government seem to have disappeared. According to Hocine, 'You couldn't begin to take shots like that today; you can't get into the working class districts. We only get to cover the most shocking news.' And even to do that, he added, they had to 'walk a fine line'.

In fact, the photographs coming out of Algeria are extremely limited. Three Algerian photographers have therefore just set up a photo agency, News Press, and are distributing worldwide through Sipa in Paris. Its manager, Ouaheb, is an old hand in the business: 'Algeria itself is in danger; why not write my name.' He goes on: 'I'll go on doing this until I die. We drink our bottle of Scotch daily as we wait. We laugh. We live.' He reckons it's still possible to work without too many limitations, and plans to set up a correspondent in every sizeable town in Algeria within the next few months – around 40 in all.

He has no doubts about the role of photography in Algeria. 'You have to shock people if you want them to act.' Show them everything. 'My photos are tough' – like the one of the small girl with her throat slit being pulled out of a well into which she had been thrown – 'people who don't believe the massacres are happening change their minds when they see them. A lot of Algerian papers that didn't use pictures much have understood, and changed their approach.'

Everyone knows that there are photos from Algeria – babies with their throats slit and burned in ovens, the heads of two small boys in a sack – too terrible to be shown. The French magazine *Marianne* published the latter on 8 September with the following caption: 'Photos from Algeria. Do you want to see them? All of them? Or would you rather have Diana?' ❏

Michel Guerrin is a journalist with Le Monde
An edited version of the article published in Le Monde *26 September 1997*
Translated by Judith Vidal-Hall

LAHOUARI ADDI

Horror behind closed doors

DAILY, Algeria beats its own record of atrocity. Women, children, the elderly are
brutally murdered in their beds to feed the climate of fear and intimidation
among the population at large. The precise identity of the perpetrators of these
crimes is shrouded in uncertainty; meanwhile, rumour is in full flight. Broadly
speaking, it falls into two camps: either the villagers are massacred by Islamists disguised as soldiers, or by Islamists in the guise of local militia men.

The victims are not killed because they are involved in the conflict between
army and Islamists; they are merely pawns in a monstrous propaganda war. Dozens of
innocent civilians die daily caught between the protagonists who hide behind the
official ban on information.

Press censorship gives them cover and impunity; allows them to kill and reap the
benefits. Delivered to their executioners in complete secrecy, the victims do not even
have the comfort of knowing that at least the world at large knows what is going on.
The public in Algeria is kept in the dark.

Why does a government which claims to support democratic values forbid access
to the local and international press corps? Why prevent them throwing some light on
the circumstances in which the entire population of villages has been massacred?
Why censorship? Who benefits? Does a free press help or hinder peace and the transition to democracy? Such questions embarrass a government whose bland, reassur-
ing press releases bear no relation whatsoever to the situation on the ground.

Denouncing the killings and expressing regret is no longer enough. It is time the
government allowed Algerian journalists to do their job in freedom, and the public
to know what is going on. Journalists are being harassed, threatened, put under pressure and subjected to constant surveillance, even in their newsrooms. What are the
authorities trying to hide when they forbid journalists to talk to survivors or describe
the massacres? Under these circumstances, every scrap of information coming out of
the country is suspect.

Censorship and the manipulation of the press creates a climate of suspicion.
People have lost confidence in the forces of law and order; they openly accuse the
government of complicity with those who slit the throats of small children. Only
freedom of information will restore the credibility of the police and army and prevent further massacres of innocents. If the present situation is anything to go by,
those who kill have no desire to be exposed to public scrutiny: they do not want the

world at large to know who they are.

The end of censorship at home and access for foreign journalists is the least one can expect from a government that has lost even the vestiges of credibility at home and abroad because of the aura of mystery that surrounds even the killings in the suburbs of the capital. Free and open communication is the only way of ending the killing: once their identity has been revealed, the assassins will not want to run the risk of losing their following. The diabolic strategy of slitting babies throats in order to put the blame on the enemy will no longer work.

Information must be 'demilitarised' and taken out of the hands of those who manipulate it. News is not a weapon of war to be used against the enemy. By keeping up censorship, denying transparency in the media, the Algerian government is a party to the crimes against humanity that are taking place in a country it claims is under its control. Sooner or later, and in one form or another, the world will demand a reckoning. Various international organisations have already proposed a commission of enquiry into the killings in the Mitidja only to be dismissed out of hand by the Algerian authorities who have invoked the principle of national sovereignty. Arguments about non-intervention in the internal affairs of a nation are relevant only when that country is threatened by clearly identifiable forces within or without. This is not the case in Algeria: the country is in the grip of an internal power struggle which has degenerated into an exchange of brutalities completely beyond the pale.

The Algerian government is sovereign only within the limits determined by fundamental moral law. When children are being murdered en masse, a government must either identify the criminals itself, or work with international bodies who can help it do so. National sovereignty is bound by natural law and common humanity. When a state stands by while a child's throat is slit, when it is unable or unwilling to protect that child, by what right does it invoke the principle of 'non-intervention' in the name of 'national sovereignty'? If a government is incapable of ensuring the minimum of civil peace and order necessary to protect its children from mass murder, it is no longer master in its own house. When a three-year-old child is murdered by having its throat slit in front of its mother, it ceases to be merely Algerian: it is the child of us all. A child at risk of death has no nationality; we are all responsible for its survival. Its premeditated murder wipes out frontiers and transcends that man-made entity 'the state'.

What point is there in keeping alive the memory of the crimes committed by the Nazis if we allow equally barbarous acts to pass unnoticed and unremarked today. ❏

Lahouari Addi left Algeria in November 1993. He is now associate professor in political sociology at the Institute for Political Studies in Lyon, France
An edited version of the article published in Le Monde *on 26 September 1997*
Translated by Judith Vidal-Hall

PHILIP JONES GRIFFITHS

No Di, no pix

IN the delirium over Di's death it may seem unwise to reveal that photographing people without asking their permission is what I do for a living.

Of course, I do my best to be low-key, unthreatening and sensitive to people's feelings. This means I've sometimes lost a picture by not lifting the camera, but it also means I've never been abused by a subject and never ever been sued over a published photograph. Generally, the only annoyance I've received from a subject is when I've either not taken a picture or not taken enough. This is fairly normal – people love being photographed.

I think of myself as a privileged observer wandering the world recording what people do, documenting social behaviour, political shenanigans and the occasional war. I strive to be as compassionate as possible and humble enough to learn. As I cannot be invisible, I try to be unthreatening and sympathetic. If I had to ask the subject every time before pointing the lens, then the person would either do something different or appear self-conscious enough to sow doubt in the mind of the viewer that the subject was somehow 'performing', making any picture worthless.

Photography is a meaningless endeavour, without veracity. People believe photographs: they regard them as true and hence their power. It's a photograph we have in our passport, not a drawing – as George Bernard Shaw once declared: 'I would willingly exchange every painting of Christ for one snapshot!' The ability of, say, Henri Cartier-Bresson's photographs to captivate, enlighten and inform relies on the fact that he photographs a 'real life' that the viewer can relate to, and not some models 'pretending'.

Picturing society, warts and all, quickly relegates the photographer to the unpopular role of critic. Unpopular, that is, with those responsible for the warts, popular with those concerned about them. The Lord Wakehams of Hogarth's day were, I'm sure, anxiously looking for ways to prevent him from exposing the plight

No one should forget that there exists a direct relationship between each cubic metre of flowers laced before the palace and every square metre of photographs printed of the princess.

of the dispossessed although, as far as I know, no one invoked invasion of their privacy!

Nowadays, the dominant 'potent' media are firmly in the hands of multi-national corporations, which control what we see and hear. Because democracies have enshrined the concept of the 'freedom of the press' in their constitutions, it is too embarrassing to be seen censoring news-gathering. By actually owning the media – and, as they say, the freedom of the press belongs to those that own one – corporate giants can regularly distort and censor news presentation to serve their requirements. As our minds are increasingly manipulated by imagery intended to subjugate us, the need for independent observers/critics is more compelling than ever.

The media moguls slipped up over Diana and they naturally want to appear eager to accept the restraints proposed by Wakeham. Restraints they will never observe, because they interfere with profits. Since when did respecting the royal family enhance Murdoch's wealth? In the meantime, the

TV newsman being attacked by police; Saigon 1968

It has been revealed that the nautical photograph of Dodi and Di was 'computer-enhanced' before publication. This is a chilling reminder that 'new' pictures are not strictly necessary. Any situation can be recreated, or even created from scratch, in a couple of hours with the aid of a computer. The tabloids' adherence to using 'real' photographs is probably more sentimental than moral.

Advertisers can be far more practical, as I found out earlier this year. Magnum, my agency, alerted me that Saatchi & Saatchi wanted to use a photograph I had taken during the Vietnam War in an advertising campaign for the British army. As a pacifist, I refused as vigorously as possible. They laughed, saying they could do without the picture and went on to recreate it using Photoshop. Naturally we sued and they settled out of court. Nevertheless, a photograph of a Vietnamese farmer, killed whilst defending his home from the invading US army, was used to persuade British youth to join the armed forces — despite permission being refused.

Wakeham proposals will act to restrict the independent observer with a camera – all in the name of protecting people's privacy.

The real invaders of privacy are big business and government. The super-computers at Visa and American Express will have known in advance what purchases Di and Dodi would have made, had they lived. And they sell this information to anyone who can pay. For every person hounded by a paparazzo, a million are photographed in their cars by police and 10 million are

video-taped in banks and public buildings. And none of those recorded want to be recorded, whereas most people pursued by paparazzi do. They employ public relations personnel to ensure that the photographers turn up at the right place at the right time.

A symbiotic relationship has always existed between personalities and their paparazzi. In today's world the famous would not be famous without exposure. For them, the more pictures, the greater the fame and power. No one should forget that there exists a direct relationship between each cubic metre of flowers placed before the palace and every square meter of photographs printed of the princess. The media inveigled the public with a torrent of hype about her, producing an appetite satiated only by ever more daring paparazzi production, which increased circulation, which in turn swelled the coffers of the proprietor. It was a closed loop in which everyone was a winner.

Diana's death requires a scapegoat. Although the verdict is not in, the photographers are considered guilty until proven innocent. One, ironically, is a colleague who risked legs, if not life, photographing victims in the minefields of Cambodia. Lord Wakeham has wacky proposals to protect privacy, proposals that include defining beaches as 'private places'! This should certainly liven them up when consenting adults with an exhibitionist streak get going.

'I did have my camera opened by a British officer in Derry after he'd seen me photographing a youth with his foot on the barrel of a soldier's rifle. Obviously, he was not protecting the soldier's privacy.'

It seems obvious to me that his proposals are the wrong answer to the wrong question. The issue of privacy is straightforward. Privacy is what you get when you are in a private place. Privacy is what you do not get in a public place. British law (up to now, at least)

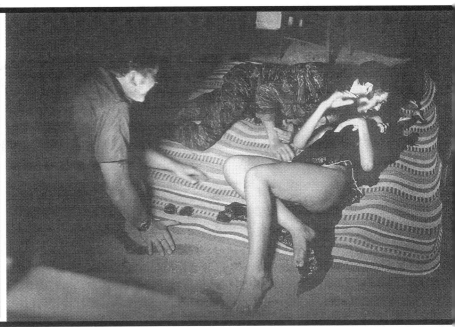

'Proud father in Cambodia, 1997 – The normal reaction of people being photographed'

recognises this in as much as there is no specific offence known as 'invasion of privacy', only trespass.

For the photographer, anything seen in 'public' can be recorded but, in 'private' the subject's permission is needed.

The logic is impeccable: if you have sex with the curtains open, you lose your right to privacy and there is no hope of successfully suing a passing photographer. But, if a photographer broke into the house to get the picture, he would be punished for trespassing and we would all cheer. ❏

Philip Jones Griffiths has been a photographer since 1961, covering the Algerian, Vietnamese and Yom Kippur wars amongst others. He is a former president of Magnum Photos.

ARTHUR DAVIDSON

Wakeham's private wars

If the Press Complaints Commission wants to avoid a privacy law in the wake of the Diana affair, it'll have to give its self regulatory code a few teeth

Privacy is the buzz word of the moment. We are told that the public is pushing for a law to protect individuals, usually popular personalities, from media intrusion. We are informed that they are incensed by the harassment of Diana, Princess of Wales and want the press to be brought to heel in some way.

Who tells us this? The media itself. We must assume that their conclusions and concerns are soundly based since editors and proprietors seem to be getting into a right old disputatious scrap about what should be done to meet the concern. Alan Rusbridger, editor of the *Guardian*, favours a limited law of privacy traded off for a relaxation of what he regards as the draconian plaintiff-biased laws of defamation. Charles Moore, editor of the *Daily Telegraph*, also favours some sort of privacy law. He seems to regard the tabloids as queuing up to see who can find the best excuse for breaching the Press Complaints Commission's code. As for the tabloids, well they don't want any truck with a privacy law. They see it as a further restriction of freedom of expression: yet another law to add to the uncertainties of the libel and contempt laws. These, they argue, already act as a serious obstacle to free and open reporting of matters which the public should know about.

Their response to the public concern which they tell us exists, is largely to blame a bunch of maverick paparazzi and fall back on the virtues of self regulation. If the code of conduct drawn up by the Press Complaints Commission (PCC) is not able to prevent what the public regard as unwarranted and unworthy intrusion into private

To boost its credibility, the Press Complaints Commission should incorporate a power to enable it to impose a financial penalty

lives, then, they say, the code must be strengthened. Lord Wakeham, chairman of the the PCC, has proposed and published a new code to meet this public pressure. Among the proposals are a prohibition on the publication of any pictures obtained through 'persistent pursuit' or a result of 'unlawful behaviour', and the establishment of a new 'overriding' public interest defence. The code is at present being discussed by the Code Committee of the PCC. It will no doubt be adopted and hailed as the world's toughest. In the short term it might even prevent the government introducing a codified or statutory privacy law. Lord Wakeham will have performed a good political job by being seen to act quickly and decisively.

But will the public be sufficiently reassured? And has Lord Wakeham acted possibly too quickly and restrictively? The public are sceptical about the effectiveness of self-regulation because the PCC has no teeth. It can apply no sanctions on a recalcitrant editor or journalist, even for a blatant breach of the code. It has firmly turned its back on any such idea. Publication in an offending newspaper of the details of the complaint against it that has been upheld, is, the Commission argues, sufficient deterrence.

It is true that editors do not lightly risk a brush with the PCC. They dislike having to publish an adverse finding. They understandably argue over, debate and refine the precise wording of the adjudication and where in the paper it is to be published. But to the public these seemingly cosy arrangements don't strike a stance redolent of contrition. Nor does it reassure them on the determination of the press to improve its standards, or its willingness to deal firmly yet fairly with those of its members who offend its own code. Too often it appears to the public to be more of a protection society, funded as it is by the press, than a body genuinely trying to be – and to be seen to be – even handed in its approach. And to some extent the press is hoist by its own petard: they are quick to criticise other institutions for the inadequacies of their self-regulation procedures, even those which, unlike the press, have the power to suspend their members or impose other penalties on them.

To boost its credibility, the PCC should incorporate a power to enable it to impose a financial penalty on those who blatantly breach its privacy provisions. This would be up to an agreed limit, say £10,000 (US$15,100) which mirrors the limit on the sum that can be awarded in defamation actions when the summary procedures of the Defamation Act 1996 come into force. This would neither be a curtailment of press freedom nor would it offend natural justice. It would be administered by its own regulatory body, not by an outside source lacking in understanding of the risks that editors must take to ensure that hypocrisy and embarrassing truths are revealed and mal-practices exposed. It would be used sparingly and only after the fullest representations had been made. In such circumstances the paper should not only be obliged to publish the findings but also a form of acknowledgement of their future and continued adherence to the code.

Lord Wakeham should seize the opportunity now to cajole and persuade proprietors, editors and, above all, members of the PCC that this is really what the public have the right to expect from a self-regulatory body which asks to be taken seriously. He would also be doing a long term service to the cause of press freedom. Sooner or later the new toughened-up code will be broken. A newspaper will publish an irresistibly exciting kiss-and-tell story with a less than credible reason for doing so. By then it will be too late for Lord Wakeham to once again suggest that the code be further toughened. By then too the European Convention on Human Rights will have been incorporated into British law. Article 8, the right to privacy, and Article 10, the right to freedom of expression, will have started being interpreted by the judiciary. In recent cases the judges have shown their intellectual ingenuity and innovative thinking by extend-ing the boundaries of the law of confidentiality, trespass and copy-right. The media should have little doubt that they can shape a priva-cy law without indulging in legalistic dishonesty. It could be that their attitudes to the difficult balancing act they would have to per-form in reconciling the right to privacy and the right to freedom of expression will be in some way influenced by the absence of a strong and viable self-regulatory system enforced by the PCC and respected by the public.

A privacy law depends for its effectiveness on prior restraint: on

Exhilarating.
Thought-provoking.
Outstanding.

To subscribe in the UK and overseas (excluding USA & Canada)

	UK:		Overseas:	
1 year (6 issues)		£38		£43
2 years (12 issues)		£66		£79
3 years (18 issues)		£96		£114

Name

Address

B7A6

£ _____ total. ❑ Cheque (£)   ❑ Visa/MC   ❑ Am Ex   ❑ Bill me

Card No.

Expiry   Signature

❑ I would also like to send **INDEX** to a reader in the developing world—just £25.
❑ I do not wish to receive mail from other companies.

INDEX, 33 Islington High St, London N1 9LH Tel: 0171 278 2313

INDEX.

To subscribe in the United States or Canada

	US:	
1 year (6 issues)		$50
2 years (12 issues)		$93
3 years (18 issues)		$131

Name

Address

B7B6

$ _____ total. ❑ Cheque ($)   ❑ Visa/MC   ❑ Am Ex   ❑ Bill me

Card No.

Expiry   Signature

❑ I would also like to send **INDEX** to a reader in the developing world—just $35.
❑ I do not wish to receive mail from other companies.

INDEX, 33 Islington High St, London N1 9LH Fax: 44 171 278 1878

INDEX ON CENSORSHIP
33 Islington High Street
London N1 9BR
United Kingdom

INDEX ON CENSORSHIP
708 Third Avenue
8th Floor
New York, NY 10164-3005

the ability of the plaintiff to obtain an injunction to prevent the truth from being published. Once the truth is out, part of the incentive publicly to pursue a legal action through the courts has gone. So the danger for the press is obvious. The bulk of applications will, of necessity, be heard in private. Vital decisions on the merits of a public interest defence, and the circumstances in which such a defence will prevail, will depend on the interpretation of individual judges. So the interests of the complainant will not necessarily be served by a privacy law and the public will be worst off in that their right to know will be further curtailed. The lawyers will benefit either through a wealthy and powerful client or through the introduction, as seems possible, of a no-win-no-fee arrangement.

The public interest is, therefore, manifestly best served by self-regulation. The public can sniff a short term political fix when they see one and they think they see one in the new code. But the public has equally shown that it will respond when those with the power to influence events demonstrate that they understand what is worrying it – and act to meet those worries. By acting in a truly statesmanlike and forward looking way Lord Wakeham has the authority and prestige to strike a blow for freedom of expression and win the support and confidence of the public in the worth of the newspaper industry's self-regulatory system. ❏

Arthur Davidson is a barrister specialising in media law and chair of the Fleet Street lawyers. He is a legal advisor to the Express Group *of newspapers. The views expressed here are his own*

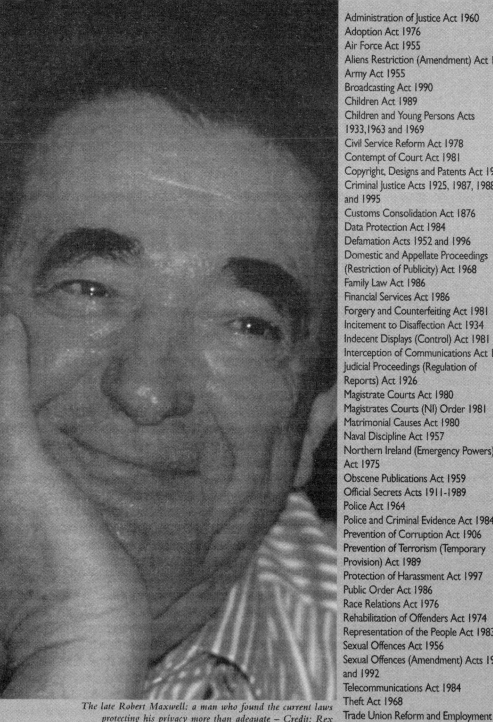

The late Robert Maxwell: a man who found the current laws protecting his privacy more than adequate – Credit: Rex

Administration of Justice Act 1960
Adoption Act 1976
Air Force Act 1955
Aliens Restriction (Amendment) Act 1919
Army Act 1955
Broadcasting Act 1990
Children Act 1989
Children and Young Persons Acts 1933,1963 and 1969
Civil Service Reform Act 1978
Contempt of Court Act 1981
Copyright, Designs and Patents Act 1988
Criminal Justice Acts 1925, 1987, 1988 and 1995
Customs Consolidation Act 1876
Data Protection Act 1984
Defamation Acts 1952 and 1996
Domestic and Appellate Proceedings (Restriction of Publicity) Act 1968
Family Law Act 1986
Financial Services Act 1986
Forgery and Counterfeiting Act 1981
Incitement to Disaffection Act 1934
Indecent Displays (Control) Act 1981
Interception of Communications Act 1985
Judicial Proceedings (Regulation of Reports) Act 1926
Magistrate Courts Act 1980
Magistrates Courts (NI) Order 1981
Matrimonial Causes Act 1980
Naval Discipline Act 1957
Northern Ireland (Emergency Powers) Act 1975
Obscene Publications Act 1959
Official Secrets Acts 1911-1989
Police Act 1964
Police and Criminal Evidence Act 1984
Prevention of Corruption Act 1906
Prevention of Terrorism (Temporary Provision) Act 1989
Protection of Harassment Act 1997
Public Order Act 1986
Race Relations Act 1976
Rehabilitation of Offenders Act 1974
Representation of the People Act 1983
Sexual Offences Act 1956
Sexual Offences (Amendment) Acts 1976 and 1992
Telecommunications Act 1984
Theft Act 1968
Trade Union Reform and Employment Rights Act 1993
Tribunals of Enquiry (Evidence) Act 1921
Unsolicited Goods and Services Act 1971
Wireless Telegraphy Act 1949

HUGH STEPHENSON

Tongue-tied

THERE are some 50 major pieces of legislation on the statute book in the UK whose effect, expressly or in practice, is to gag journalists. The latest example is the 1997 Protection from Harassment Act. In time, this could become a partial and back door Protection of Privacy Act.

A cloud much larger than a man's hand hangs over the media in the shape of next year's Data Protection Bill, designed to implement by 1998 the corresponding European Union directive. The bill would turn the present Data Protection Registrar into a Commissioner with new powers to require those holding data to inform the individuals concerned what data is being held about them and why; and to introduce safeguards – like an obligation to obtain prior consent over the use of sensitive personal information – with wider compensation for those who can show that the regulations have been broken in their case. In its present form, the legislation would signal the end of any kind of investigative journalism in the UK. ❏

Hugh Stephenson is professor of journalism at London's City University

CHRISTOPHER HIRD

Myths, lies and the royals

In Britain, we are not able to read of royal pecadilloes in Kitty Kelley's latest kiss-and-tell-all, *The Royals*. The UK media and publishers have seen to that. With the deference that has characterised its relationship with the crown since time immemorial, the press has conspired to belittle and diminish a book that undermines long held establishment shibboleths. In the interest of public debate on a subject long kept under wraps, and with no need for unsubstantiated gossip or the more malicious tittle-tattle of the streets, *Index* shows another side of the story.

THE smart thing is to sneer at Kitty Kelley's *The Royals*, a book which is not available in British book shops. There's Professor Ben Pimlott in the *Guardian*: 'an audacious practical joke...as cold as a dead grouse... anybody looking for new information should cancel their ticket to the US to purchase a copy... historical method is not Ms Kelley's forte.' Or Professor David Cannadine in the *London Review of Books*: 'A book so bad that Britons cannot realise how fortunate they are in being unable to buy it: wholly lacking in historical perspective or context, saying little that is new or interesting, devoid of any coherent argument or overall interpretation, prurient in its obsession with human weakness and written in prose that makes tabloid journalism seem almost fastidious.'

Let's hope there's a touch of irony here. Or does Cannadine really believe that a lack of historical perspective or possession of an interest in human weakness should be grounds for keeping the published word from those of us who are not the authors of books characterised by their concern for historical context and an abundance of footnotes? And perhaps we should be interested in the personal failings of a family promoted to us for most of the postwar period as a paragon of virtue and a model of family life; not because these are their failings as such, but because they expose the gross hypocrisy of the royal family's position.

The tenor of most of the criticisms of the Kelley book has been that of the knowing insider: we all know that they are unfaithful in marriage; that the Duke of Windsor supported the fascists; that they are boorish and virtually incapable of normal human relationships. In recent years, even the most casual reader of the newspapers couldn't miss some of this. But even if you have a sense of it, you may be short on the detail. And there is a lot about the royal family that *will* only be known to those who have read virtually every book that has been written and have assiduously stored press cuttings from the tabloids. If you haven't done this, then Kelley's book will tell you something you didn't know.

The vast number of books on the royal family make it very hard to

The odd couple? – Credit: Tim Rooke/Rex

know how far Kelley's book relies on other people's work and the lack of precise sources is an irritation if you want to play hunting the source. But, this apart, it's a wonderful book. You cannot read this book without agreeing with the Queen Mother's description of herself: 'You think I am a nice person, I'm not really a nice person.' She is not at all nice – and neither are any of her family. Kitty Kelley, I am sure, is no revolutionary; but she comes from a republican political tradition. What is so appealing about this book is that it displays no sign of being touched by the mystique of royalty – a mystique which still infects so much written by British authors about the monarchy and the royal family.

One part of this mystique – largely undamaged by anything which has happened in the last 15 years – is the powerful bond between the British people and the royal family during World War II. This book paints a rather different picture. 'The King and Queen sidestepped the country's strict food rationing and regularly ate roast beef and drank champagne. Butter pats were monogrammed with the royal coat of arms and dinners served on gold plates.' While London restaurant prices were controlled, the King 'ordered two eggs and six rashers of grilled bacon for breakfast every day and grouse in season for dinner every night.'

And when the war came to an end, while Britain was living off ration books, Princess Elizabeth was living in luxury. 'While her future subjects were still restricted to clothing coupons and wearing skirts made of curtains and trousers cut down from overcoats, she had her own couturier and was ordering strapless satin evening gowns.' The royal family received an extra 160 clothing coupons – on top of the 66 which ordinary mortals received; and when they went on a tour of South Africa after World War II, they were issued with a staggering extra 4,329 coupons. The royal family's privileged treatment during rationing is not, it is true, a Kelley discovery; it is well known to the millions who have read an article by Dr Ina Zweiniger-Bargielowska in a 1993 edition of *History Today*, a source Kelley acknowledges.

The scale on which the Queen lives is breath-taking, especially when set against the well polished image of her as frugal. In November 1950, at a time when hardly anyone in Britain could afford a foreign holiday, Princess Elizabeth took a three-month trip to Malta. 'Accompanied by her maid, her footman and her detective, she arrived on the island with her sports car, 40 wardrobe trunks and a new polo pony for her husband.' The next year, when she went to Canada, she took 189 wardrobe trunks.

Where the royal family are careful with their money is in the pay of
their servants. As John Barratt, former secretary to Lord Mountbatten says:
'All the Windsors are as mean as cats' piss.' Christmas presents to servants
were blow heaters, bath mats and, from Princess Margaret, a lavatory
brush. In 1993, as public indignation about the royal family's wealth grew,
the Queen economised: by making her £5,600 a year chauffeur pay for
his shoes and her even less well paid servants pay for their own soap. This
notorious meanness is also well chronicled in another book, it too
unavailable in Britain, *The Housekeeper's Diary* by Wendy Berry, (Barricade
Books, NY 1995).

Prince Charles persuaded the British courts to ban the publication of
Berry's book in Britain on the grounds that she had breached her contract
of employment. It's a pity that we cannot publish information from it
because the book provides fascinating insights into these people's lives and
behaviour. It is easy to see why Charles was so keen to keep this book
banned: it showed that the contract which was being broken was that
between him and his subjects. But the move came from a long tradition in
the royal family of keeping the public in ignorance of what they get up to.
The Queen Mother stopped Princess Margaret's footman publishing a
book on some of the more arcane habits of Anthony Armstrong-Jones;
the Queen prevented the *Sun* from publishing the memoirs of an aide
which chronicled Prince Andrew's one night stands. And where the royals
leave off, the British libel laws take over.

When the courts are not available to the royal family, they lie. As
George VI was dying, the Queen Mother rouged his cheeks for public
appearances, to disguise his illness. The palace staff were told to deny that
this was happening. During the 1950s, the Queen was a great gambler,
twice topping the list of money-winning owners. The official palace line
was she loved horses, but never gambled. In 1973, they said that Princess
Anne and Mark Phillips had never met – in fact, they were just about to
get engaged. And, as we now know, they lied again and again about the
state of Charles and Diana's marriage. When a police guard at Highgrove
truthfully stated that they slept in different rooms, it was categorically
denied. When the Andrew Morton book about Diana came out it was
denounced as 'preposterous'. As the recent edition confirms, it was deadly
accurate.

But the palace was not alone in attacking the Morton book: most of
the British establishment and its friends in the media – including the Press

Complaints Commission – joined in. Today, these attacks on the veracity of Morton's work make them look extremely stupid. But, then as Kelley chronicles, the British press has a long tradition of complicity in keeping up the image of the royal family.

When Prince Charles visited the Taj Mahal – whilst engaged to Diana, but continuing an affair with Camilla Parker Bowles – he said, 'I am encouraged by the fact that if I were to become a Muslim I could have lots of wives'. None of the accompanying press corps reported this. When the Queen told reporter James Whittaker to 'Fuck off', he reported it as 'Go away.' When Prince Philip asked the *Independent* to excise a section of an interview, in which he described the former French President, Vincent Auriol, as 'a frightful buggerer', they agreed.

These may seem small matters; collectively they illustrate how, until recently, the British press did not want to tell the truth about the sort of people who sit on or near the throne. Are people familiar, for example, with some of Princess Margaret's comments? According to Kitty Kelley, she described *Schindler's List* as 'a tedious film about Jews'. And said of the President of Guyana: 'He's everything I despise. He's black; he's married to a Jew; and, furthermore, she's American.' She and her husband asked for a US$30,000 appearance fee for a US charity fundraiser; she returned a friend's Christmas present in exchange for cash.

Then there's Kelley on Diana's homophobia: sacking most of the gay employees because she didn't want them around her sons; her suggestion that Prince Andrew's father is really Lord Porchester; her description of the Duke of Edinburgh hitting a US government driver because he refused to take orders from the Duke rather than the US secret service; and how the royal family's obsessive dislike of divorce meant that the Queen tried to stop Jackie Kennedy asking her sister to dinner because she was divorced?

In view of subsequent events, this particular obsession has some piquancy. But then the royal family's attitude to marriage and sex is, by most people's standards, unusual. Prince Philip had a string of relationships (often with people passed on to him by Lord Mountbatten) before he got married to Princess Elizabeth – an event which proved to be only a temporary hitch in his scheme of things and which was not, on his part, a result of being in love.

Kitty Kelley makes allegations that, during the 1950s, Philip and two other men calling themselves 'the Three Cocketeers', 'entertained' young actresses; and that he had assignations during a four-month tour on the royal yacht Britannia, one of which left a daughter in Melbourne. If this was the case, it makes Charles's attitude to women more understandable. He also had a marriage of convenience, which did not really interfere with his relationship with Camilla Parker Bowles. She spent nights with him on the royal train during his engagement and within weeks of his marriage he was back with her.

The Royals: on sale everywhere except the UK – Credit: F Fisher

Largely because of the sex stories, this book will not be published in Britain. It's a pity because – as Diana said of Charles: 'He's supposed to be a paragon to people. He's going to be the goddamned Defender of the Faith.' The British monarchy has the most remarkable capacity for self preservation and reinvention and you can be sure that no effort will be spared in the next few years to try and re-establish some of the mystique. The power of this book is that it so comprehensively undermines this and reveals the emptiness of the monarchy's claim to be an upholder of any sort of decent values. If there is only one book you read about the royal family, make it this one. ❏

The Royals *by Kitty Kelley (Warner Books) Price US$27 in the USA; not for sale in Britain*

Christopher Hird *is a journalist and TV documentary producer*

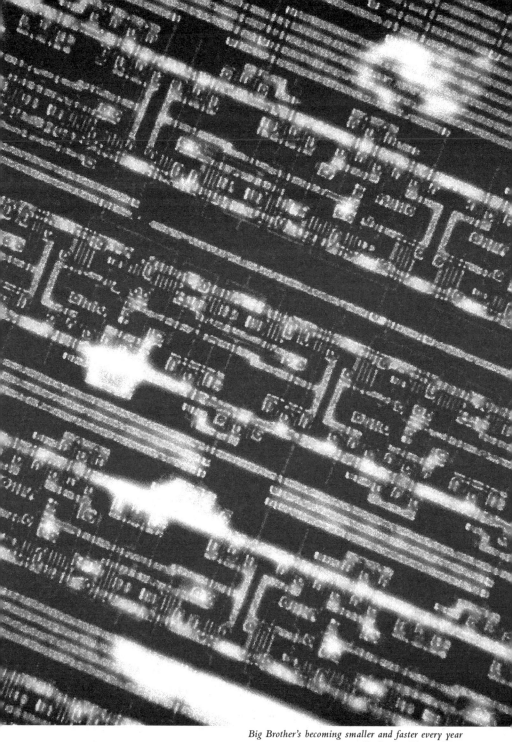

Big Brother's becoming smaller and faster every year
– Credit: Jon Tarrant/Rex

SIMON DAVIES

Time for a byte of privacy please

Digital technologies – like video cameras, DNA profiling, satellite surveillance, police systems and credit reporting agencies to name but a few – have created the potential for invasions of privacy and rights on a scale that could scarcely have been imagined even 20 years ago – and the threat to everyone's privacy increases daily

GOVERNMENTS are fond of arguing that rights are not static. Times change. Civil disobedience, they say, creates a need for a reduction in the right of assembly. The Internet necessitates a review of the right of free speech. Organised crime requires a fundamental revision of property rights.

Media are equally fond of promoting these arguments. In the reasoning of so many press organisations, the balance of rights which our parents enjoyed has little relevance to the pressing concerns of today. Changing technology and changing human behaviour require us to constantly review the extent of individual liberties.

This view is valid only in rare circumstances. Human rights must rest on a solid and meaningful foundation, or they will perish. Revision so often leads to erosion. If there exists a valid argument for decreasing rights on the basis of public interest, there is a far more valid argument for routinely reviewing and strengthening rights when individual liberties are threatened. Numerous rights are in need of such reinforcement - and none so urgently as the right to privacy.

Whenever civil rights advocates discuss the destruction of privacy, they usually frame their concerns around the growth of surveillance. And these days, surveillance depends on information technology.

The range of new technologies, and their almost limitless spectrum of functions, is creating a buoyant surveillance economy. Rapid advances in video and audio interception equipment, identification technologies and intelligence-gathering systems have created an unprecedented sweep of opportunities for police and security agencies. Surveillance has become a fixed component of the burgeoning information economy. Each adult in the developed world is located, on average, in 200 computer databases.

The next generation of technology will exploit a growing fusion between people and technology. An intimacy without parallel will mean that areas of life traditionally considered private will be comprehensively revealed. Technological convergence will ensure that all machines will, in time, have the ability to communicate with each other.

A Global Information Infrastructure – potentially the greatest force since the birth of the automobile – is being forged. Mass surveillance is developing from Argentina to Zambia not merely through video cameras, DNA profiling, satellite surveillance, police systems and credit-reporting agencies, but through a vast range of computer-based surveillance mechanisms. Even now, mobile phones and bank machines create a real-time geographical tracking mechanism. Search engines on the internet present a detailed picture of people's activities and interests. Data matching allows authorities to link computers from different areas of the public and private sector. And the advent of this surveillance society will bring with it a new era of social control. The two have always existed hand in hand.

In a recent article in the *Guardian*, press baron David Barclay, proprietor of the *European* newspaper, warned 'the need for our protection as individuals has never been greater'. He proposed that 'a right to privacy should deter all forms of intrusion into...an "inner circle" inside which someone may live his personal life as he chooses.'

So it is with privacy and the media. This generation has seen a significant increase in media intrusion. New technologies create the potential for invasions of privacy and rights on a scale that could scarcely have been imagined even 20 years ago. Indeed, the threat from media to everyone's privacy increases daily. Digitisation – the conversion of words into electronic bits – means that data from media organisations soon becomes available in many 'machine readable' forms that can be analysed, duplicated, stored and transmitted. Globalisation ensures that the process occurs worldwide. Combined with powerful database search facilities, the effect on people's lives, happiness and reputation can be devastating. Media make use of these technologies of surveillance and should not apply one rule to government, and another to themselves.

The argument for better privacy protection against this combination of forces should be compelling. And yet, the death of Princess Diana highlighted a rare consensus among media throughout the developed world: privacy laws are inimical to a free society. The Press Complaints Commission, which enforces the current regime of self-regulation in Britain, also opposed privacy legislation. Commission chairman Lord Wakeham disregarded his own patchy track record in controlling press intrusion by advising: 'Some people are trying to let the privacy genie out of its bottle.'

In his article, David Barclay drew a rare link between the realm of traditional surveillance by police and other authorities, and modern media practices, but stopped well short of supporting a statutory right. 'The abuse of press power,' he concluded, 'is unacceptable. I believe that far worse, however, would be a new statute law in Britain that interferes with the freedom of the press. Barclay advised that such a law would invite an abuse of power by the state, and the subsequent threat of dictatorship.

Privacy rights should not be bought off so cheaply. The issue of privacy protection is not merely about paparazzi and the famous. It is about ordinary people in extraordinary situations. AIDS patients, families of disaster victims, the children of people in the news, members of political parties – all have a right to lead their lives without harassment. Those who have served their time in prison, or those wanting to run the gauntlet of justice with some dignity, have a right to privacy. Gifted children, pregnant women, animal lovers and train enthusiasts do, in certain circumstances, find themselves the target of unwanted media intrusion – no matter how well intended it might be. Interesting stories that spring from the lives of these people, and millions like them, cannot be used as part of a public interest defence against a right to privacy.

What, after all, would be the practical effect of a right to privacy? Perhaps some of the worst excesses of so-called 'investigative' journalism will have to change. But in most circumstances the law would merely reflect existing codes of conduct of journalists' associations. The argument by Lord Wakeham, Rupert Murdoch and others, that rich and powerful people will use the new law to gag press reporting is a red herring. The media seem to pay scant attention to internal threats, such as press monopolies, conflicts of interest, gratuities, self-censorship, editorial accountability and standards of reporting. The threat of control through a piece of legislation appears to exercise the interest of the media more than the threat of injunction and judicial process.

The European Convention of Human Rights, soon to be incorporated into British domestic law, accords privacy and freedom of speech as equal rights. In our modern society they are compatible, not conflicting. Those who seek to set one against the other are serving self interest before the public good.

I believe there are legislative solutions to suit the twenty-first century and that we should strive to agree on those solutions. All of us – privacy advocates and media professionals – are working to create a fairer society, governed in a more transparent and accountable way. ❏

Simon Davies is director general of Privacy International and a visiting fellow at the London School of Economics. He is the author of Big Brother *(Pan 1997)*

EUROPE-ASIA STUDIES
Formerly
SOVIET STUDIES
EDITOR
Roger Clarke, *University of Glasgow, UK*

Europe-Asia Studies is the principal academic journal in the world devoted to the political, economic and social affairs of the former Soviet bloc countries and their relationship with the rest of Europe and Asia.

Volume 50, 1998, 8 issues. ISSN 0966-8136.

For your free inspection copy contact:
Carfax Publishing Ltd ● PO Box 25 ● Abingdon ● Oxon OX14 3UE ● UK
Tel: +44 (0)1235 401000 ● *Fax:* +44 (0)1235 401550
E-mail: sales@carfax.co.uk ● WWW: http://www.carfax.co.uk/eas-ad.htm

---

India, Pakistan, Bangladesh: Partioned

India and Pakistan celebrated 50 years of Independence in som-
bre mood. India's president chose to castigate the corruption
that stains his country's democratic record; in Pakistan, the
army still rides roughshod over that country's tentative democratic recovery. In both countries, the return of sectarian confrontation is a reminder of the violence of Partition that accompanied freedom in 1947. It was an aspect of Independence that
most chose to forget. Index recalls the voices from that time,
reflects on the continuing legacy of Partition – and looks at the
experience of thrice partitioned Bangladesh

File compiled with the help of Urvashi
Butalia and Radha Kumar

EQBAL AHMAD

The price of freedom

In both India and Pakistan, the fiftieth anniversary of Independence was anticipated with high expectations. In the event, the anniversary passed quietly. Official celebrations were muted, and citizens in both countries expressed more doubt and discontent than patriotic fervour. The promise of a peaceable South Asian future may lie in this awareness of common failure

INDIA divided on the eve of decolonisation. What Pundit Jawaharlal Nehru called its 'tryst with destiny' was marred by widespread violence and the largest known migration in human history, involving at least 15 million people in just about 90 catastrophic days.

Partition did not resolve the problems it aimed to solve. Rather, the problems of ensuring the rights and representation of minority groups, and of containing expressions of religious and cultural chauvinism have been vastly augmented by a host of new impediments to the common weal. India and Pakistan have fought three wars and carried on an exorbitant arms race which now includes nuclear bombs and missiles. Full scale war may break out again as the two countries' armed forces come to blows almost weekly across the Line of Control in Kashmir, and their secret services engage in a savage exchange of sabotage and support for violent sectarian groups. Their open hostility barely masks the identical failure of India, Pakistan and Bangladesh to provide for the basic needs of citizens for food, employment, transport, housing and education. A rigid post-colonial order perpetuates a system of virtual apartheid to cushion the contented few from the sorrows of the overwhelming majority of the sub-continent's deprived people.

The ironic silence on Bangladesh during this fiftieth anniversary is indicative of our anxieties about the future. Bengali support of the Muslim League played a crucial part in the Partition of India. But within two decades, Bengalis became alienated from Pakistan and, after violent convulsions and an Indo-Pakistan war, seceded in 1972 from the country they had helped create. India supported then East Pakistan's secession. But it too has been beset by separatist demands in the north-east, in Punjab and in Kashmir, where nationalist insurgency and India's efforts to suppress it have cost upwards of 60,000 lives. As did the Kashmiris under Sheikh Abdullah's leadership, the Sikhs had supported the Indian National Congress against the Muslim League, and opposed the creation of Pakistan. Three decades later, Sikh nationalists sought Pakistani support in their struggle against the Federal Government of India. The case of Bangladesh, and also of Punjab Sikhs and Kashmiri Muslims, suggests that nationalist identity is fluid by nature. It is shaped less by history and 'ancient hatreds' than by contemporary forces and events.

The post-Partition uprisings in East Pakistan, Punjab and Kashmir suggest that Indian and Pakistani ruling establishments ignored the lessons of Partition, chief among them, the forest fire speed with which ethnic and religious conflicts spread. Until almost the end of the 1930s, Muslims tended to support the Indian National Congress or provincial parties other than the Muslim League. Mohammed Ali Jinnah, Pakistan's founding father, was himself a leading Congress leader once, and widely regarded as an 'ambassador of Hindu-Muslim unity'. In the first Indian elections of 1937, the League garnered a mere four per cent of Muslim votes. Yet three years later it formulated the demand for Pakistan, and in 1947 achieved it.

An enquiry into how so dramatic a turn-around occurred suggests that the majority leaders' failure to comprehend the anxieties and insecurities of a minority people can speedily lead to their alienation. In the age of nationalism and mass politics, alienation is likely to translate into the demand for 'self-determination' and separate statehood. There is a premium in heterogeneous environments not merely on goodwill but also on statesmanship. The Partition of India was a product of the key modern forces of colonialism, nationalism, the growth of a modern state structure and the promise of representative government. Right-wing Hindu ideologues often portray Muslims as violent conquerors fundamentally alien to India. VS Naipaul is to my knowledge the first well known writer to ply this view. In a leading article in *India Today*'s

Partition in the Punjab 1947: Muslim refugees head for Pakistan
Credit: Illustrated London News

anniversary issue (18 August 1997) he argues that India 'was ravaged and intellectually destroyed' by Muslim invasions from about 1000 AD, and it was not until the 'British period, and in the 50 years after the British period, [that] there has been a kind of recruitment or recovery, a very slow revival of energy and intellect.'

Muslim hate-mongers hold a similarly manichaean view of India's history. But there is little in the centuries-long history of Hindu-Muslim relations to anticipate the demand for and creation of separate statehood. An overwhelming majority of the subcontinent's Muslims were indigenous people who shared the languages, cultures, and historical memories of their Hindu or Sikh neighbours. They were converted to Islam not by the sword but by social movements including the Sufis, who were widely revered in the countryside by members of both communities.

Conquests, ancient or modern, are not pretty things. Tyrants – Rajput, Turk, Mughal and English – did torment Indians at various times. Also, tension and conflict between Hindus and Muslims did occur, as they did within communities and across caste boundaries. Similarly, communal violence occasionally broke out especially at proximate sites of ritual observation. Yet, organised communal violence was rare until the beginning of the twentieth century when it began to make its appearance in urban areas. Great Britain, the colonial power, pursued a policy of 'divide and rule', and remained committed to it until it had lost the will to rule and decided to 'divide and quit' in a haste that was irresponsible and costly in human lives, property and sheer mayhem.

But divide-and-rule policies were not the only divisive factors associated with colonialism. There was also the contrast in Hindu and Muslim responses to the colonial encounter which placed them on differing scales of modernity. For a variety of reasons, Muslims shunned western culture and education for nearly a century and did not begin to acquire modern knowledge until the latter half of the nineteenth century. After the suppression of the 1857 revolt, India formally became a crown colony. The event heralded, among other developments, the organisation and expansion of a modern state and the steady growth of a native 'salariat' to serve it. The state, not a growing capitalist economy, was the parent of India's middle class, its nurturer and provider. The culture of this middle class, its outlook and aspirations, jealousies and competitive spirit were shaped by the requirements and promises of serving the state. Muslims, who had earlier shunned modern education as western and colonial, now eagerly sought it. Thus, the first western-influenced, reformist Hindu movement – the Brahmo Samaj led by Raja Ram Mohan Roy – preceded its first Muslim counterpart – Sir Syed Ahmed Khan's modernist movement – by nearly a century.

The effects of this contrast in the nature of Hindu and Muslim responses to the West were dialectical; therefore far reaching. In the colonial administration, Muslims were latecomers and under-represented. It followed that they also lagged in founding and joining modern political parties and in articulating nationalist demands. Among the Muslim upper and middle classes of the 1920s and 1930s, there was a sense of anxiety at having fallen behind, an anxiety which accentuated as the promise of independence and democratic rule appeared increasingly realisable. Their first instinct was to seek guarantees of minority representation in government and politics. When these were not conceded sufficiently by the dominant party – the Indian National Congress – some Muslims would turn to alternatives: to class and confessional formations.

Maulana Abul Kalam Azad, two-term president of the Congress, was the most popular Muslim leader until Jinnah wrested Muslim support from him. The Maulana would later ascribe this turnabout to the Congress leaders' failure to show generosity toward the defeated Muslim League in 1937 by inviting their participation in the many provincial governments which the Congress led. The failure of the Congress leadership lay also in not recognising the class clout of the Unionist landlords in Punjab, the mobilising power of AK Fazlul Haq's peasant populism in Bengal or the Muslim League's ability under Jinnah's leadership to make tactical alliances and compound its power and influence.

In the period between the world wars, as the colonial state expanded and opened the doors of its superior civilian and military services to Indians, the competition for jobs became broader, more intense and more political. The British policy of establishing quotas on the basis of religion and castes underlined the importance of jobs in the state sector, and also legitimised the expectation of communal claims on the resources of the state. As the prospect of self-rule increased, so did the competition for representation in and control over the state.

Beginning with the Morley-Minto Reform Act of 1909, India made gradual advances toward representative government. By 1935, it had become obvious that within a decade or two India would be self-gov-

erning at least as a British dominion if not as an independent state. The
Muslim minority viewed the prospect of self-rule and democracy with a
mix of hope and anxiety. Broad-based Muslim support for the Congress
in the 1937 election was an expression of the hope. Their rapid turn
toward the Muslim League in 1939-1940 marked the arousal of anxiety.
The gap between hope and anxiety was widened by a rival nationalism,
elements of which had become integral to the Muslim League as well as
the Congress although the latter was, in principle, a non-communal
party.

From its beginnings, Indian nationalism had three divergent streams:
secular, Hindu and Muslim. Such early nationalists as Aurobindo Ghosh
and later Bal Gangadhar Tilak not only employed Hindu religious symbols but also portrayed the Muslim, along with the British, as the Other.
Mother India, they claimed, had been the victim of both. Muslim
nationalism, on the other hand, drew on the pan-Islamic rhetoric and
symbols which were in vogue during the late nineteenth and early twen-
tiethcenturies throughout the Middle East and North Africa.

Secular and communal nationalism often resided in the same individual. Tilak was both a Congress leader and a Hindu nationalist.
Mohammed Iqbal, the poet, wrote nationalist as well as pan-Islamic
poems. In Pakistan, he is honoured as a founding father while in India's
Republic Day celebrations, its armed forces 'beat the retreat' to the tune
of an Iqbal poem. The communal strains of nationalism coexisted for a
time inside the Congress, converging under the umbrella of secular
nationalism.

Mahatma Gandhi presented a most remarkable instance of such convergence when he joined Maulana Mohammed Ali to lead the Khilafat
movement, an anti-British agitation in support of the Ottoman caliphate
which had hardly any defenders left even in Turkey. This political gesture
was in complete harmony with Gandhi's style of deploying cultural and
religious symbols and themes as a means to mobilising the masses in the
struggle against colonialism. Ironically, it was Jinnah who warned against
such a spiritualisation of Indian politics. He was right. For the amalgamation of religious and secular motifs and ideas reinforced a sectarian
outlook among Muslims and Hindus alike. As India approached independence, leaders with a sectarian outlook and sentiments such as Sardar
Vallabbhai Patel and Rajendra Prasad had gained commanding positions
in the Congress. Mohammed Ali Jinnah was already leading the Muslim

League which formulated in 1940 the demand for a separate Muslim state.

Was the partition of India inevitable? It is too early for a definitive answer. I believe, nevertheless, that India could have remained united but the price would have been the centralised colonial state. Since the end of World War 1, Jinnah had been proposing decentralisation of power as a way to defuse minority fears and make independent India more governable. But as nationalists everywhere have been prone to do throughout the nineteenth and twentieth centuries, India's leaders, too, equated national unity and good governance with centralised power arrangements.

The last opportunity to save India's unity was presented by the Cabinet Mission Plan of 1946 which envisaged a loose federation with a relatively weak central government. Both the Congress and the Muslim League accepted the plan. Then the Congress had second thoughts, expressed by Jawaharlal Nehru. Jinnah, known by then as the Qaid-i-Azam, decided to protest against this rejection with a 'Direct Action Day' which passed peacefully elsewhere in India but in Calcutta ignited large-scale communal violence. Mass level violence occurred next in the predominantly Muslim district of Noakhali, then a communal carnage happened in Bihar, a predominantly Hindu province. In all three instances, Congress and Muslim League leaders co-operated to end the violence. Mahatma Gandhi campaigned at length to restore communal peace in Noakhali and Bihar. But the fire spread with astonishing speed. Large-scale violence rendered the partition of India a certainty.

Barely half a year later, on 3 June 1947, the partition plan was announced. Congress and Muslim League leaders ignored the dire warnings of Calcutta, Noakhali and Bihar when they acquiesced in Lord Louis Mountbatten's callous and mindless haste to become Britain's last Viceroy in India. The fire then took hold, devouring all in its way, including Mahatma Gandhi. ❏

Eqbal Ahmad is a Pakistani writer and academic

NAILA KABEER

A thrice-partitioned history

The partition of a nation is generally accompanied by the simultaneous evocation of notions of identity as the basis of its separate components, and of difference to rationalise their separation

B ENGALI Muslims have been through three partitions since the start of this century. Not all have been equally traumatic but each has in turn illustrated the shifting definitions of interests which bring about partitions and the shifting notions of identity and difference through which they are expressed.

The Bengali Muslim experience also bears witness to the fact that the mobilisation of identity as the basis of community can be as violent, as bloody and ultimately as lethal as the establishment of difference for the basis of separation.

The first partition of Bengal took place in 1905 under British rule and resulted in the amalgamation of East Bengal and Assam into a separate Muslim-dominated province. It was justified by the imperial powers on grounds of both administrative convenience and the separate interests of Bengal's Muslims from those of its Hindus, but it has also been interpreted as another example of British divide-and-rule tactics in India. It was opposed by a combination of high-caste Bengali Hindus whose landed interests in East Bengal were directly undermined by the partition as well as by prominent Muslims who responded to appeals to unity on the basis of a common Bengali language, literature, history, tradition and way of life. It was annulled in 1911.

The second partition took place in 1947 when India itself was divided at the moment of its independence from British rule. The new state of Pakistan was set up as a homeland for the Muslims on the subcontinent. East Pakistan – Muslim-dominated East Bengal – was separated by over 1,000 miles of hostile Indian territory from West Pakistan which consisted of Baluchistan, Sind, North-West Frontier Province and Muslim-dominated West Punjab. Thus, what is generally referred to as the Partition of 1947 was in fact two geographically separated partitions:

'Sonar Bangla': the free and 'golden' Bengal of poets and people – Credit: Heldur Netocny/Panos

the partition of Punjab and the partition of Bengal.

The partition of Punjab was characterised by massive migrations of Hindus and Sikhs into India and of Muslims into the new state of Pakistan within a very short period of time. One of the most enduring and potent symbols of the 1947 Partition are the trainloads of the dead which travelled in both directions, migrants massacred as they made their way to a refuge on the 'right' side of the Punjab border. After this single convulsive moment of exchange, all movements appeared to grind to a halt for the next half century as the borders were effectively sealed off between the two Punjabs.

The Bengal partition of 1947, as Joya Chatterjee has pointed out, was both different and perceived as so by the Indian authorities. In Bengal, the worst communal massacres occurred in 1946, the year before, but Partition itself did not result in the catacylsmic violence, rapes, abductions, forced conversions and trainloads of dead which feature in descriptions of the Punjab partition. There were no massive movements across the Bengal border in 1947 and no forced conversions. The Bengali Hindus who did migrate to India, both in 1947 and since then, were not perceived by the Indian authorities to be fleeing from the same levels of religious intolerance in Muslim Bengal as those from Muslim Punjab, and hence were not received by the authorities as casualties of Partition in the same way. The borders of partitioned Bengal, although policed on both sides, have remained more or less open since Partition. I know because I crossed them them every year between 1956 and 1965 on my way to and from boarding school in an Indian hill-station.

Whatever the truth of the two partitions, differences between Muslim Punjab and Muslim Bengal introduced a fundamental cultural bifurcation into the identity of an already physically bifurcated new state. West Pakistan had rid itself of its religious minorities in one convulsive moment in 1947 and now constituted an almost purely Muslim community. In contrast, a sizeable minority of Bengali Hindus lived and continued to live in East Pakistan – around 15 per cent of its population – and there appeared to be a great deal of overlap between the cultures of Bengali Hindus and Muslims, breeding suspicion about the authenticity of Bengali Islam among West Pakistanis.

As a nation that had come into existence as a homeland for the Muslims of the subcontinent, Pakistan was bound to justify its existence in terms of its separate Muslim identity and hence needed to purge itself

of any Hinduised remmants from its past. With the increasing dominance of Punjabis in the ruling apparatus of the new state, it became
clear that it would be *their* version of Islam and hence *their* version of
Pakistan that would dominate.

The first evidence of this came in the early attempt to impose Urdu,
a language widely spoken in West Pakistan, as the official language of the
new state and, when this failed, to introduce the Urdu script for the
Bengali language. The defence of Bengali became the rallying cause for
Bengali nationalist sentiment: within a year of partition, East Pakistan
had an active Language Movement and, within five years, its first martyrs
as the police opened fire on students demonstrating in defence of their
language.

In 1954, the Muslim League, the party that had fought for Pakistan
before Partition, was resoundingly defeated in East Pakistan and never
had a presence there again. The elections were won by the Bengali
Muslim Awami League who dropped the epithet 'Muslim' and hence-
forth became the voice of the disenfranchised Bengali middle classes. To
ensure that the Bengali population could not gain a political majority in
government by virtue of its numerical majority in the country, the four
provinces of West Pakistan were reconstituted as 'One Unit' in 1956 and
given parity of electoral representation with East Pakistan. Along with
the introduction of indirect forms of electoral representations to keep
Bengalis out of political power, fiscal and monetary measures were introduced to transfer the economic surplus out of East Pakistan to finance
industrialisation in West Pakistan.

Although East Pakistan won the language issue, the drive by central
government in the western wing to forge a national identity as different
as possible from its past continued. A Bureau for National
Reconstruction was set up to purge the Bengali language of Sanskrit
(read Hindu) elements and to purify it with apparently more authentical-
ly Islamic words from Arabic, Persian and Urdu. The songs of Tagore,
much loved by Muslim and Hindu Bengalis alike, were banned from
state-controlled radio and television, restrictions imposed on the dissemination of Bengali literature and grants offered to artists and literati who
were prepared to work for 'national integration'. A policy of assimila-
tion-through-miscegenation was adopted in the 1960s in the system of
incentives offered to inter-wing marriages.

In the face of this depiction of their 'Bengaliness' as somehow not quite Islamic enough, Bengalis began to assert their cultural differences from West Pakistan, a process which led to the politicisation of normally uncontroversial aspects of everyday middle-class life. The right to sing the songs of Tagore, to wear the saree and the *bindi* (the red mark on the forehead indicating a married woman) customary among Bengali women, the more relaxed attitude to the idea of the daughters of the middle classes singing and performing in public, all activities which had once appeared commonplace, became acts of dissent in a context in which they were regarded as evidence of the 'Hindu aberrations' of Bengalis.

In fact, the dress and deportment of Bengali women took on increasing symbolic value in the struggle to assert cultural difference. One of the most powerfully remembered images in Bangladesh today of its struggle for national autonomy is that of the thousands of women wearing the yellow sarees with red borders associated with celebration, wearing *bindis* and singing songs of Bengali nationalism – including the banned songs of Tagore – who were in the vanguard of the massive demonstrations which began to take place in Dhaka in the final years of East Pakistan.

The break-up of Pakistan is easy for later generations of Bengalis to understand, but not why the country ever existed in the form it did. Was it a breathtaking leap of the imagination, or a devastating failure, to believe that that two peoples, separated from each other literally by over 1,000 miles of enemy territory and symbolically by culture, language, history, apparel, diet, calender and even by standard time, could ever constitute a single nation simply on the grounds that they shared a common religion? The policy of attempting to redefine one wing in the image of the other was one way to bridge this divide but it was doomed to failure. When the 'One Unit' federation of West Pakistan was finally dismantled in 1970 and direct elections held, it looked like the inevitable fears of the ruling elite were about to come true. As they did when the Awami League swept most of the seats in East Pakistan and won an overall majority in the country.

But the inevitable was not allowed to happen. Instead, in March 1971, the Pakistan army moved into East Pakistan and unleashed nine months of genocide and rape on its people in the apparent belief that this would rid them of their nationalist aspirations. We are, of course, more aware now how often rape is used as a weapon of war. Some feminists see it as the logical expression of men's inherent violence towards women. Some scholars see it as an attempt by one group of men to dishonour another group of men by highlighting their failure to protect their women. The Pakistan army brought a unique additional element of 'holy war' to its acts of rape against over 30,000 Bengali women: it saw it as part of its mission to populate the region with 'pure' Muslims. The terrible inner logic which had driven the earlier policy of assimilation-by-miscegenation was laid bare by the war. A third partition, this time of Pakistan, was inevitable and Bangladesh declared its independence, choosing as its national anthem a much loved song by Tagore, '*Sonar Bangla*'.

The truncated Pakistan that remains continued to struggle with notions of identity as other cultural aspirations that had been suppressed in its struggle to dominate its eastern wing came to the fore. Aside from the older struggles of the different provinces in the face of Punjabi hegemony, new divisions have arisen. One such is with the *Mohajirs*, those who migrated, mainly in 1947, from all over the subcontinent as refugees to Pakistan, and who eventually began to coalesce around their own political interests within the country. Anwar Iqbal, a journalist whose family had migrated from India first to East Pakistan in 1947 and then to West Pakistan in 1970 as a gulf began to open up between the Bengali and non-Bengali population, writes about the confusing politics of what it means to be a Pakistani today: 'Although dozens of ethnic and racial groups live in Karachi, the main division is between *them* and *us*. The definition of *them* and *us* varies from group to group. If you are a *Mohajir*, a Muslim immigrant from India, for you all non-*Mohajirs* are *them*. If you are old Pakistanis, then the *Mohajirs* are *them*. But sometimes even that is not clear. One group of *Mohajir* can become the real *us* and another the real *them* for each other, depending on their party loyalties. Similarly, the older Pakistanis can divide themselves into various ethnic groups such as the Punjabis, the Sindhis, the Pashtoon and the Baluch and treat each other as *them*.'

A drive towards further Islamisation has been the most striking feature of post-1971 Pakistan. A variety of new religious ordinances were brought in, many of which discriminated explicitly against women and minorities. The Ahmediya minority was constitutionally declared non-Muslim in 1974 and a number of religious ordinances, drawn from the *sharia*, over-ride rights given to women under civil law. Today, with increasing violence between Shia and Sunni Muslims, Pakistan is distinguished as the only place in the subcontinent where Muslims kill Muslims, even within the sanctuary of the mosque, *because* they are Muslims or, more accurately, because they are the *wrong sort* of Muslims.

For Bangladesh itself, the main problems since 1971 have related to economic hardship and political stability; poverty and the defence of democracy. However, questions of identity appear sporadically on the political agenda, if only because successive military rulers turned politicians have resorted periodically to Islam and to appeals to anti-Indian sentiment to shore up their political support. Indeed, it seems to be indelibly imprinted in the imagination of this breed of rulers that to be Muslim necessarily means to be anti-Indian, and often, by extension, pro-Pakistani.

At the same time, however, Bangladesh has managed to avoid declaring itself an Islamic Republic and enshrining *sharia* law in its legal system. Consequently, the rights of women and of minorities have been safeguarded and, while there are episodic and often terrible violations of both, they are not sanctioned by the state; and the state can, and has been mobilised to deal with them. Family courts have been set up all over the country to ensure that women have quicker recourse to justice than would be the case if they were required to go through the main legal system. Women are emerging from the home to take up factory work in cities, sometimes out of poverty and sometimes in search of economic independence. Bangladesh's Grameen Bank has innovated the practice of lending without collateral to the assetless, particularly women, and has been emulated as a model for the reduction of poverty in countries of the North as well as the South. Primary and secondary schooling have been free for girls since 1992, something which may explain a remarkable closing of the gender gap in education. Finally, not only has the country had two women prime ministers in quick succession but the present one appears to be performing the extraordinary feat of being simultaneously pro-Indian and pro-Pakistani.

Partitions lead nations to re-invent their histories so that their stories of the past can be brought into line with their sense of the present. Many Pakistanis would prefer to deal with their past by simply blotting out any memory of the events of 1971 because those events undermined the very principle on which Pakistan was founded: as a place of safety for the Muslims of the subcontinent. And many of those who do remember choose to remember the creation of Bangladesh as a product of Indian machinations to dismember and thereby weaken its old enemy, Pakistan.

However, as long as successive generations of Pakistanis continue to accept this selective reading of their past, rather than trying to learn from it, their country will continue to be torn apart by the violent politics of identity. They need to remember that far from being 'not-good enough' Pakistanis, the Muslims of Bengal were in the forefront of the movement for Pakistan. The Muslim League was founded in East Bengal in 1906 with Bengali Muslims playing a dominant role; it was the Bengali Muslims who gave the Muslim League its first and only electoral victory in the provincial elections of 1937 and its first opportunity to form a Cabinet; the Muslim League won again in Bengal in 1946; the 1940 Lahore resolution which called for the setting up of Pakistan was moved in the Muslim League by a Bengali Muslim, one of the leading members of the Muslim community in India at that time.

Just as important, is the need for them to remember the role West Pakistan played in the processes which led to the creation of Bangladesh. India may have had its own reasons for supporting the aspirations of the Bengali Muslims for national autonomy in 1971, but those aspirations were called into being by the bigoted, bungling and, in the end, murderous elites of Pakistan. ❏

Naila Kabeer is a fellow at the Institute of Development Studies, Sussex, UK. Her latest book The Power to Choose: Bangladeshi Women Workers in London and Dhaka *is due shortly.*
She would like to thank her uncles Farhad Ghuznavi and Rezaur Rahman for their help with this article.

URVASHI BUTALIA

More hidden histories

*O*FFICIALLY, *Partition has been forgotten in India, its painful memories put aside. No mention is made of it in government documents, and its enormous, long-term human costs do not figure in histories of the subcontinent. Unofficially, however, these histories live on, inside families and communities, and are told and retold: people recall the time when, suddenly, neighbour turned upon neighbour, friends became foes, boundaries were suddenly set up, and whole lifetimes of sharing had to be put aside and new, hostile identities assumed. Communities separated into 'them' and 'us', religion became the marker of identity, borders were suddenly drawn across villages and communities.*

These are the many hidden histories of Partition, the things history books don't tell us about. In the 10 years or so that I have been working on Partition, it is these histories that I have listened to, these that have led me to realise how this cataclysm affected the lives of ordinary people, those who live on the margins of society — women, children, the poor, untouchables. In each of the stories I listened to, there was a different telling, a different experience.

There are hundreds of such histories: histories that tell us that Partition was not only about being Hindu and Muslim, it was about being a harijan *[untouchable], a woman, a child; about love and sharing, about friendships. Only when we begin to listen to the stories of Partition's survivors shall we begin to understand: only through the cracks in the official version do we find the human actors who are the real stuff of any history.*

In August 1947, Mangal Singh and his two brothers took a decision they would remember all their lives: to kill 17 of their family members — mostly women and children — so that they would not run the danger of being converted to Islam. Calling everyone together in the family house, the brothers then took up the *kirpan*, the sacred sword of the

Sikhs, and, as each person 'offered' herself for death, 'martyred' her. Their task completed, the brothers made good their escape to Amritsar across the newly determined border in Indian Punjab. Their own village was no longer safe: it had become part of Pakistan, on the 'wrong' side of the partition.

Several years after Partition, I asked Mangal Singh — by then the only survivor of the three — about this. Why kill only the women and children? Did they not deserve a chance to escape? And how had he coped with the grief, the burden of such a painful memory? He refused to accept the word 'kill', insisting on 'martyred': because they were weak, because the women would have been forced to convert or would have been polluted through rape by men of the other religion. And his own grief?

> 'Hunger drives all sorrow and grief away. You understand? When you don't have anything, then what's the point of sorrow and grief? If you don't have anything in your stomach, you can't even cry. It's not easy to forget. One doesn't forget, but it's time that dictates to you. No-one...will...wipe away your tears, wake you from sorrow.'

Mangal Singh's fear was not unfounded. Thousands of women were raped and abducted by men of the 'other' religion (and often by men of their own) in the course of Partition. Often families decided to do away with their women in order to 'save' them from this fate. These women then became martyrs to the 'cause' of religion. Basant Kaur was one of 90 women who jumped into a well to drown themselves rather than fall victim to the aggressors. She did not die: by the time she jumped in, the well had filled up with bodies. She remembers the time:

> 'Many girls were killed. Then...Mata Laajwanti...she had a well near her house, in a sort of garden. Then all of us jumped into that...I also went in. I took my two children, and then we jumped in. I had some jewelery on me, things in my ears, on my wrists and I had 14 rupees on me. I took all that and threw it into the well, and then I jumped in...but it's like when you put *rotis* (bread) into the *tandoor* (oven), and if it is too full, the ones near the top, they don't cook. They have to be taken out. So the well filled up and we could not drown.'

Damyanti Sahgal was a social worker, who worked in camps that had been set up to house the hundreds of women who were recovered after abduction by men of the other religion. In September 1947, when the scale of the abductions became clear (some 75,000 women are thought to have been abducted on both sides, a figure that does not include Kashmir for which no statistics were available), the two countries mounted an operation to recover women. Once found, these women would be housed in transit camps, in the care of female social workers, and their families would be contacted, so that the women could be restored to them. Several complications arose: often, the women would refuse to go back to their families. They had lived with their abductor for some time, they had children by him, at times they even had a better life with him than in their own homes. And then there were the families who, in turn, refused to take their women back because they felt they had been polluted through sexual contact with men of the other, the enemy, religion. Damyanti recounts how the abducted women were hunted down:

'In the mornings we used to go to find girls from the rural areas...we'd go selling eggs...into the villages. And we'd ask people for *lassi* (buttermilk)...then we'd say we have come from Hindustan [as refugees] and you know, my younger brother, these bastard Sikhs have taken his wife away... He is bereft and lonely. Do you know of any daughter of *kaffirs* [a Hindu woman] in this area? If there is any such girl, do tell us, maybe we can buy her; and the poor man, at least he can set up home again.'

Anis Kidwai, who worked with Muslim women, explained why, in her view, many abducted women were reluctant to be 'recovered' and did not want to return:

'There were some women who had been born into poor homes and had not seen anything other than poverty. A half full stomach and rags on your body. And now they had fallen into the hands of men who bough them silken salvars and lace dupatttas, who taught them the pleasures of cold ice cream and hot coffee, who took them to the cinema. Why should they leave such men and go back to covering their bodies with rags and slaving in the hot sun in the fields? If she leaves this smart, uniformed man [large numbers of women were actually abducted by the police and army] she will probably end up with a peasant in rags...and so they [the women] are happy to forget the frightening past, or the equally uncertain and fearful future, and live only for the present.'

If women faced rape and abduction, their children, legitimate or otherwise, also became victims of this history. Kulwant Singh was 11 at the time of Partition.

'I was small. My mother, when she saw my father being killed – they cut him up into 100 pieces – the first blow they struck on his neck, and then they cut him into 100 pieces...at that time I was trembling, at my feet there were many bodies, there were fires all around. I was dying of thirst, they heard my voice. My mother lifted me from my head and my aunt took my feet. The six-month-old daughter, first of all they did *ardas* [prayed] and threw her into the fire, and then they said, "Bibis, our izzat is in danger, will we save our honour or our children?" And then turn by turn they threw their children into the fire...my mother, she took me and put me down by my father's body, where there was fire all around, and I felt so thirsty and because of the heat, my legs got burnt.

'[Later] I got up. My hands were cut, blood was flowing from my body, my body was burnt. I fell down...I was walking on thorns, huge thorns, but at the time I could not feel them.'

Maya Rani has a story of another kind. A sweeper in a school in Batala, Maya was 16 at Partition. Sweepers belong to the untouchable caste – officially outside the pale of mainstream society. But, in this case, it was this very 'disadvantage' that worked to her advantage.

'Weren't we frightened? No....all the children of that area, none of us was scared. Often we would leave our own roof and climb onto a neighbour's, just to see. Then we all got together and started to go into people's houses. In some we found rice, in others almonds...we began to collect all these and pile them up in our house...

'I kept lots of utensils, *hamams*, and all for my wedding. I brought a lot of utensils with me when I got married. I also looted many quilts...there were 11 of us girls, we all made our dowries with the stuff we collected...'

How did she and her friends escape the violence?

'We thought, who's going to take us away, who's going to kill us? We call ourselves *harijans* [children of God]. Hindus, Christians, no-one can take us away.'

Partition was not only a history of rape and murder. It was a history of friendships that have endured, of love and sharing, and of regret, regret for violence, the enmity that suddenly stared people in the face. In December 1947, Chaudhry Latif, a Muslim refugee from India, received a letter addressed to him as 'The Occupant' of his new house in Lahore, Pakistan. It was from Harkishan Singh Bedi, the earlier occupant of Latif's home. 'I write to you,' Bedi said, 'as a human being...we are human beings first and Hindus and Muslims only after that.' For many years Latif and Bedi kept up a correspondence: Bedi described where he had kept his precious books and papers which Latif meticulously collected and sent in small packets to him. ❑

Urvashi Butalia is an Indian writer and publisher. She is a founder of the publishing house Kali Books for Women. Index published the first of her 'hidden histories' in Index 4/1995

Partition 1947: Sikhs and Hindus flee divided Punjab for the Indian side
Credit: Illustrated London News

Songs of Partition

Our poems from India, Pakistan and Bangladesh explore partitions of thought, emotion, intellect: between people and within relationships; between ideas of the traditional and the modern; of exile, loss and dislocation. They cover a broad spectrum of generations and origins and a few of the many languages of the subcontinent.

Selection compiled by Sudeep Sen

Rabindranath Tagore – India

Where the mind is without fear and the head is held high;
Where knowledge is free;
Where the world has not been broken into fragments by narrow domestic walls;
Where words come out from the depth of truth;
Where tireless striving stretches its arms towards perfection;
Where the clear stream of reason has not lost its way into the
dreary desert sand of dead habit;
Where the mind is led forward by thee into ever-widening
thought and action –
Into that heaven of freedom, my Father, let my country awake.

From *Gitanjali* – *Translated from Bengali by Andrew Robinson and Krishna Dutta*

Shamsur Rahman – Bangladesh
Crows

No footprints on the dirt track
No cow or cowherd in the pastures
The ragged dykes desolate
Roadside trees hushed and all
Around in naked sunlight
Crows flapping wings, crows, only crows.

Translated from Bengali by Kaiser Haq

Faiz Ahmed Faiz – Pakistan
Ghazal

The heart a desecrated temple
   in it all statues of you broken
Those forgotten sorrows
   my memories of you return
gods abandoned by their worshippers
One by one by one
   the stars light up the sky
In step with them
   you approach me in the dark
   your final destination

Tonight increase the pace
   with which the liquor is poured
   Oh tell the drummer to play a breathless beat
Worshippers have abandoned the mosques
   they're coming here to the wine house

It is the night of waiting
   tell her let no more time elapse
This pain of longing may dull
   already my memory is beginning to blur
   at any moment I may forget her

Translated from Urdu by Agha Shahid Ali

Kaiser Haq – Bangladesh
The Border

Let us say you dream of a woman,
and because she isn't anywhere around,
imagine her across the border.

You travel hunched and twisted in a crowded bus,
on a ferry through opaque night
lacerated by searchlights

to this squalid frontier town:
a one-legged rickshawallah takes you round

to a six-by-eight room, the best in the best hotel.

But instead of crossing over you lie dreaming
of a woman, and the border:
perfect knife that slices through modest households,

creating wry humour – whole families
eat under one flag, shit under another,
humming a different national tune.

You lie down on the fateful line
under a livid moon. You
and your desire and the border are now one.

You raise the universal flag
of flaglessness. Amidst bird anthems
dawn explodes in a lusty salute.

Alamgir Hashmi – Pakistan
On Hearing that the Wall in Berlin

has come down in part, I went
to acknowledge a little sentiment
about its coming down a bit
before going back up again
to keep those behind it on either side
clear about their attachments,
of the difficulty without it
to look across –
forty years of building; a political art
that divides the heart from your heart:
a little regret, a certain loss.
Maybe it's too late for some.
Even dying were easier than some divisions –
when the holes made into the future
hold no light; even driving out at dawn
it is dark in your particular lane.
Now we can think of the walls that remain;
recess in the brickwork, love that is gone.

Gulzar – India
Communal riots

No man has hacked in the city;
those were only names
that were murdered,

Nobody beheaded anyone;
only the severed hats
had heads in them.

And the blood
you see on the streets
belongs to the butchered voices.

Translated from Hindi/Urdu by Rina Singh

Mahendra Solanki – India
Slaughter

We offer a sacrifice, a goat
Stunned into two by a sword.

A ritual made real by blood;
An act to make us whole.

Memory

This refusal to dislodge the past:
forever her face in repose,
before any animation or sound;
as if held in a vaselined lens.

Moniza Alvi – Pakistan
Map of India

If I stare at the country long enough
I can prise it off the paper,
lift it like a flap of skin.

Sometimes it's an advent calendar –

each city has a window
which I leave open
a little wider each time.

India is manageable – smaller than
my hand, the Mahanadi River
thinner than my lifeline.

Sudeep Sen – India
During the Street Play

In the cobbled quadrangle
rises a primitive voice:

clear, and elemental.
His figure, draped in raw linen,

carrying a staff.
Others, black-robed, masked,

gradually close in
in concentric circles,

repeating after him the lines
in a choral refrain

He is not Moses
the shepherd from Egypt,

he is not even a politician
campaigning for the next season.

He is, perhaps, just a local
student, the rights of humans,

maybe even a little justice.
The stage, very simple.

A quadrangle, this time,
but it could be

a market-place next time,
a street corner, a college campus.

The street-lamps spotlight the act,
or the sun will do if it is day.

The daily-wear is a fine costume,
the play quite straight-forward,

about you, and us,
about now, and in real time.

But that is too much
for the government.

Soon the police arrive,
dismantle the props, oust

the actors, as they exit
protesting in words.

*For Safdar Hasmi, the political playwright killed on the streets of Delhi
1989 while performing* 'Hulla Bol'

Mohammad Nurul Huda – Bangladesh
Sleepers born of the same mother

And then
the two born of the same mother are unperturbed, deep in sleep.
A little ways off the sea's lullaby takes in the whole horizon.
The beach's sand heaped like the jasmine flowers.
The earth is an improvised cot on bearers' shoulders galloping to eternity.
The sky-*chador* swells up like the wind in a sail.
And then
the two eternal sleepers have no separate beings;
Man or fish, animal or plant,
They could be anyone.

Translated by Carolyne Wright with the poet.

Women protesting about the death in custody of Kashmiri separatist Ahmet Beig
Credit: Martin Adler/Panos

FURRUKH KHAN

A legacy of violence

PARTITION, rather than Independence, is the defining moment in the
modern history of the Indian subcontinent. The bloody price of
freedom paid by Muslims, Hindus and Sikhs is still largely unacknowl-
edged. Yet the memories of that cataclysmic event continue to dominate
the social and political policies of both India and Pakistan.

No sooner was the announcement of Independence and Partition
made public, than the scattered but widespread religious-ethnic conflict
took on a more ominous form. Communal violence, of a type never
before experienced in India, was unleashed to speed the ethnic-cleansing
that would purify the land of the new nations. In the months following
the creation of Pakistan, the largest human migration in the history of
mankind took place. By some estimates, over 16 million people crossed
the newly created borders; over 1 million of them lost their lives.

In the frenzied attempts to despoil and dishonour the departing citi-
zenry, women's bodies assumed the burden of the chastity, purity and
honour of each community, now become separate nations defined above
all else by religion. The scars of this sexual violence against women continues to be repressed and deliberately ignored by the community at
large.

Not so much out of natural revulsion to the barbarities of that time,
more perhaps because the mass rapes and forced abductions, public
humiliations and murders were not, as it is most often claimed, carried
out by small groups of *badmashs* (criminal characters), but were, according to eye witness accounts of the time, the work of quite ordinary people who have since been reintegrated back into their communities.

Even though the violence was in one sense indiscriminate against
men and women, the latter quickly became the target on both sides of
the Hindu–Sikh/Muslim divide. In the nationalist struggle for
Independence from Britain, India had been portrayed as a female deity

in the form of Mother India. She it was who sustained her people and who must now be rid of the foreigners ruling her. Images such as these, as well as many others put the woman at the centre of the struggle for freedom. With Partition, the rhetoric of Independence that had urged the restoration of the honour of Mother India, split and turned in on itself: now, in defence of its own national honour, each side set about dishonouring the women of the enemy.

Over 100,000 women were kidnapped or forcibly taken away from fleeing families. There are hundreds of eyewitness accounts of mass rapes and murders of women. In some cases, especially among the Sikh community, men 'martyred' their women and children rather than running the risk of their being 'dishonoured' by the Muslims. There are accounts of women, naked and shaven, being paraded in public places before being killed. Over 100 Muslim women were paraded thus in the grounds of the Golden Temple in Amritsar in the Punjab, the Sikhs' holiest shrine, before they were killed.

Like the attacks by Serbs and Croats on Muslims in former Yugoslavia, such atrocities are designed to create rifts in the social and family structures of the victims that long outlast the events themselves. Eyewitnesses recall that while being tortured or raped, women were taunted by their tormentors with the failure of their menfolk to protect them, sowing doubt in the minds of the victims about the manliness, courage or concern of the men of their families and of the community in general. The public and particularly brutal nature of the humiliations also shames men and women alike into silence. But the most damaging and far-reaching aim of systematic attacks on women is to impregnate as many as possible thus destroying the myth of the purity of their community. On their return home, those who had survived their ordeal and escaped their attackers often suffered a second time. Widely stigmatised as fallen women, many were rejected by their own families; others continued to bear the shame of being dishonoured.

In Pakistan, the state has fostered a reluctance to talk about these shameful events that lasts to this day. Immediately after Partition it urged the nation to put all its energy into the newly independent Pakistan: anything that threatened to divert attention from that prime task was discouraged. As a result, any discussion of the women's ordeals was suppressed and, with the passage of time, society as a whole is either unaware of or unwilling to talk about the collective pain of its women.

Fifty years on, the painful legacy of Partition continues to work its way out in Pakistan. Successive governments, dominated by the country's feudal patriarchy, appear to have believed that if something is not talked about in public, it will go away. As a nation, we have yet to look at our own past, along with its blemishes, rather than the one created and sustained by the government and those with vested interests.

Pakistani society, collectively, has linked the notion of the dishonour of its women to the 'honour' of the nation as a whole, and has refused to confront these difficult and painful experiences – precisely, one might argue, as their perpetrators intended. One consequence, at least, is the impunity enjoyed by the growing number of men who carry out violence against women, in public places as much as in the privacy of their own homes. Pakistani women are more at risk today than ever in the short history of their country. And this time the threat is not from men of another tribe, another country, another religion, but from within their own families.

Domestic violence is successfully used to curb any attempts by women to achieve any role or identity other than that imposed by their menfolk: the narrow, socially-assigned roles as mothers, sisters or wives. Almost universally, sexual or individual identity is denied by the family as well as by society and state.

By imposing its own highly selective and acceptable version of the past on the country, the state has afflicted Pakistanis with an equally selective amnesia: the role of their women, their sacrifices, their pain in the past may be recalled – but 'they' are not allowed to talk about their experiences today.

The ghosts of the past have not been exorcised and manifest themselves in many forms of violence. As well as the brutality against their women, there is the ethnic and religious rage that is threatening to engulf Pakistan as it celebrates its fiftieth birthday, and which may yet divide the country against itself. ❏

Furrukh Khan is a doctoral student at the University of Kent, UK

SALIL TRIPARTHI

The march of Vishnu

A new wave of Hindu nationalism with its intolerant demand for a return to a remote and mythical 'golden age' of Hindu dominance is threatening all who stand in its way

A S INDIA celebrates the fiftieth anniversary of its Independence and, more important, the survival of its democracy – perhaps its greatest achievement in the post-war era – an illiberal wind is blowing across the Indian plains. What began as a mild breeze has gained squall-like ferocity as the overwhelming Hindu majority has begun to take issue with works of art, pieces of journalism, literature, opinions and political comment that offend it. This undermines Hinduism's long-held claim to tolerance, and newly-emboldened politicians, professionals, academics and journalists criticise what they characterise as the 'knee-jerk, pseudo-secular' view of India. They demand a common civil code for all, and oppose the 'appeasement' of any minority group.

All of which is part of legitimate discourse in a democracy; except that free expression has become a casualty in the process. As the state has atrophied, vigilantes, special interest groups and others with narrower identities and sectarian views, are becoming the arbiters of common taste and decency, creating a new wave of communally-enforced censorship that derails free thought and discussion. Ironically, some of the most outstanding proponents of Hinduttva – the new, militant brand of Hinduism – have themselves become the victims of this climate. Arun Shourie, a leading civil libertarian turned Hinduttva columnist finds that politicians of virtually all hues (with honourable exceptions) would like to ban his searching biography of the late Babasaheb Ambedkar, leader of the Untouchables, whom many Indians regard as the father of the present secular, social democratic constitution.

For many years, the Hindus have watched while other communities sought bans: Parsis demanding the blackening of a photograph of a Zoroastrian funeral in Dom Moraes's *Bombay*, published by Time-Life; a 'Council of Vigilant Parsis' objecting to Cyrus Bharucha's film, *On Wings of Fire*, which they labelled 'repulsive'; Christians angrily protesting against the staging of *Jesus Christ Superstar*, or arguing in public with Melvyn Bragg (who wrote the screenplay) at the British Council in Bombay; the Kerala Catholic Association demanding a ban on *Kristhuvinde Aaram Thirumurivu*, a Malayalam play based on Nikos Kazantzakis's *The Sixth Sacred Wound of Christ*; and, in the most well-known case, Muslims demanding a ban – and worse – on Salman Rushdie's *Satanic Verses*. (India was the first country in the world to ban the novel outright).

The trend continues: in September, a district court in Kerala was to hear a petition filed by a Syrian Christian lawyer who sought a ban on 1997 Booker Prize winner Arundhati Roy's acclaimed novel, *God of Small Things,* on the grounds that it was likely to cause inter-caste trouble.

Now, Hindus, incensed by what they perceive as persistent slights on their faith, are striking back in kind. Some are upset that *Fire*, a film by the Canadian-Indian film-maker, Deepa Mehta, that raises the hitherto ignored issue of lesbianism in a conservative, middle class north Indian family, has not only been centred on a Hindu family, but that the two women are named Radha and Sita, model women and heroines of the historic Hindu epics, *Mahabharat* and *Ramayan*. Other Hindus are bothered by the film *Bandit Queen*, based on the life of Phoolan Devi, female dacoit turned politician, because it shows upper caste Hindus in a poor light. Yet others are angry with Meera Nair's latest film *Kama Sutra*, which, they claim, depicts an aspect of ancient India best left on the walls of the temples of Khajuraho or confined to the privacy of the bedroom. And Shiv Sena politicians are so angry with 'pseudo-secular' journalists that they have sent storm-troopers to pillage the offices of *Mahanagar,* a Marathi daily in Bombay which has consistently opposed and exposed their party.

This Hindu hypersensitivity is a relatively new phenomenon, and instructive about the state of the world's largest democracy. Subject to certain 'reasonable' restrictions, India's liberal constitution guarantees the fundamental right to life and liberty and the right to free expression. With few exceptions, the courts have sided with the artist, the writer, the journalist, the performer, against the state which seeks to ban their work.

It is a well established tradition in Indian jurisprudence: in the late 1970s, the police sought to ban playwright Vijay Tendulkar's *Sakharam Binder*, on grounds of obscenity, but Justice Madhukar Kania overruled their decision. In 1982, when the Shiv Sena wanted to prevent Pune's Theatre Academy from taking its controversial play, *Ghashiram Kotwal*, to Berlin, the judiciary ruled in favour of the play, saying that the play was a work of art. It did, however, require that the group read a statement aloud before each performance abroad, stating that the play was fiction, and the group complied. Again, in 1988, when film-maker Govind Nihalani made his stunning television series *Tamas* (Darkness) based on Bhisham Sahni's novel about the violence during the 1947 Partition, a Muslim businessman, intriguingly backed by the youth wing of the Hindu Bharatiya Janata Party, sought a ban on the series. Again, the court ruled

Early Hindu nationalists – Credit:
Börje Tobiasson/Panos

in favour of the film.

While these liberal traditions were being upheld by the judiciary and the press, a much weakened executive had begun to cede its authority to special interest groups, allowing them to dictate what could and could not be discussed in the public domain. For instance, feminist organisations have succeeded in inserting a clause in India's already quite rigid film censorship guidelines that makes possible the banning of films which display women 'in ignoble servility to men'. At least one film has been banned on these grounds; and the tearful, angry producer of another such vented his frustration by physically jumping on and single-handedly destroying the Fiat car belonging to a member of the board of censors who ruled his film should be banned.

Lawyers, usually upholders of free expression, have also cried foul: in the film *New Delhi Times*, an editor-husband jokes to his lawyer-wife: *Vakil to sab jhoothe hote hai* (All lawyers are liars). Outraged lawyers succeeded in getting the sentence deleted from the film in states with less liberal censorship boards.

Police authorities too have been restive with film-makers who have, not entirely erroneously, shown constables or inspectors drunk on duty, corrupt or brutal sadists. While some of these films, like Govind Nihalani's *Ardh Satya* (Half-truth), have been accurate and gripping, others, the products of Bombay's *masala* film industry, lack any artistic or social significance.

Finally, politicians have taken umbrage and used the power of the state legislatures to intimidate the media. In 1987, PH Pandian, then speaker of the Tamil Nadu state legislature in southern India, took advantage of rarely-used provisions governing Contempt of the Legislature to jail S Balasubramanian, editor of *Ananda Vikatan,* a satirical Tamil magazine, for publishing a cartoon. Under a picture of two identical men sitting on a stage, the caption asked: 'Which of these is the MLA (Member of the Legislative Assembly) and which the minister?' Answer: 'The one who looks like a pickpocket is the MLA, the one who resembles a thug is the minister.'

Explaining his decision to the members of the legislature, Pandian was unusually candid: 'Don't hold any brief for filthy journalists. It is I who protect you. We're not Englishmen, we are Tamilians wearing *dhotis* not suits. Try making fun of a pedestrian and see the consequences. You may be ready to lose your reputations, I can't.'

In one sense, the cartoon hits at the heart of the problem in India today – the struggle between the 'gentlemen' and the *dhoti*-clad; between the one who follows Queensbury rules and the one who is a street-fighter. It is the tension between India and Hindustan, between Bombay and its reincarnation as

Mumbai. It is the discord between those who swear by and want to abide by the constitution, and those who don't want to waste time reading it – or worse, who can't read.

A new, more real India is on display here: where parliamentarians are not the lawyers of the 1950s and early 1960s, but often people with a criminal record; men who are more likely to hurl abuse at their opponents – at times the paperweight – than seek to win them with sophistry.

As the modern Indian Republic begins the second half of its first century, this debate can only get sharper. Does India want to live by its 1950 constitution which has created a liberal, secular, socialist, democratic republic? Or will it seek to return to a more glorious past? To its critics that past is narrow and feudal; to the believers it is the age of Ram Rajya – the mythical reign of Lord Rama – shorthand for a time when crime was non-existent, peace reigned and people were happy. More and more Hindus are becoming convinced that they need Ram Rajya and are expressing their atavistic longings more openly.

The last decade has emboldened those who were wavering. Between 1986, when the movement to build a Hindu temple on the spot where some believe Rama was born began, and its culmination, six years later, in the destruction of the ancient Muslim Babri Masjid which sat on the supposed site, the Indian polity has changed and, with it, the nature of political debate.

As the Hinduttva brigade became noisier, the Congress government – which had enraged middle-class opinion across India by shamelessly overturning a court judgement which would have allowed Muslim women the right to maintenance after divorce and rendered them equal with all Indians before the law – lost power in the 1989 elections. Television serials based on *Ramayan* and *Mahabharat* were watched by mesmerised millions on state-run television and car stickers extolling Hinduism became ubiquitous. A Bombay cricket pitch was dug up to prevent a test match between India and Pakistan from taking place; Hindus, armed with *trishuls* (tridents) and waving saffron flags, marched to the beat of loud drums. Director Alyque Padamsee, who staged his version of *Cabaret* around that time, concluded it with two small children, acting as thought police, dressed in Nazi attire – but in saffron colours – leading away the guilty. Censorship – of thought, behaviour and talk critical of this form of Hindu fundamentalism – was the next, inevitable step.

When Hindus outnumber other communities by four to one in a country of nearly one billion, this Hindu muscle-flexing is dangerous. If Muslims can get *Satanic Verses* banned, and if Christians can try to get *The God of Small Things* banned, what is to stop Hindus marching against Ambedkar's *Riddles of*

Hinduism which questions some Hindu practices?
Incremental incidents such as these build into a collective crescendo which threatens the democratic, secular republic. As economist Amartya Sen has pointed out, it is India's democracy that has ensured that while it may not have become a richer nation since Independence, its poor have not died of starvation, a compelling refutation of the self-serving logic of rulers in southeast Asia who argue that dictatorship alone ensures the masses are fed. In 50 years India has become a net exporter of food without draconian China-style measures; and, while human rights violations occur almost daily in India, there are concerned Indians within India working against them who are neither in jail, nor mere poster-boys for human rights groups. There is no Indian Wei Jingsheng, Pramoedya Ananta Toer nor Aung San Suu Kyi.

India's greatest achievement in the last 50 years has been in effectively refuting the argument, propounded by apologists of Asian values, that you have to be rich before you can be democratic: that you must be wealthy before you respect individual rights. However, in the pursuit of Lakshmi, Hindu goddess of wealth, some Indians are beginning to think that the liberal constitution has become a liability.

True, the economic pie hasn't grown fast enough, and economic liberalisation since 1991 has accentuating inequities. It is against this background that the seductive logic of Hinduttva, that seeks an outsider to blame for today's problems and finds a handy scapegoat in the 'enemy within' – the Muslim who invaded India centuries ago and transformed the Ram Rajya into a nation of paupers – continues to win supporters. As the strength of the Hindu militants grows, people will begin to talk in whispers, swallow their words and retreat into silence. That would be India's greatest tragedy.

India has always had a syncretic, inclusive nature. Rajasthani kings hired Muslim artists to paint the *Ramayan;* Shah Jehan used Hindu artisans to build the Taj Mahal. Husain's painting of a nude Saraswati can scarcely offend a society with a thousand-year-old tradition that depicts nude gods and goddesses in intimate attitudes.

Perhaps it is indeed time for India to rediscover that once-glorious past, where art flourished, and artists did not have to hide from a mob; where, to recall the poet Rabindranath Tagore's words, 'the mind is without fear and the head is held high' ❑

Salil Tripathi, formerly a correspondent for India Today, *is now southeast Asian economic correspondent for the* Far Eastern Economic Review

SALIL TRIPARTHI

Sarasvati unleashed

ON a cool December evening in 1996, the old Sir Cowasji Jehangir Hall
in downtown Bombay gleamed once more, as in the city's post-
Independence heyday. Painters, art critics, and socialites mingled with col-
lectors and the state governor in Bombay's first international class art gallery,
the latest addition to India's National Gallery of Modern Art.

The inaugural show was dedicated to the Progressive Artists Group,
founded in 1948 by six painters and sculptors – MF Husain, SH Raza, HS
Gade, SK Bakre, FN Souza and KH Ara – who set out to create an artistic
idiom for a newly-independent India. In the years that followed, Bombay
became the centre of liberal, secular, urbane, cosmopolitan discourse.

With the hall returned to its pristine glory from its humbler years first as
a venue for boxing bouts, subsequently as a cheap bargain basement empori-
um, one might have thought the
golden days of Bombay had
returned. Not so. In 1993, the
city had witnessed ruthless rioting and, by 1996, was a different
city with a different name –
Mumbai.

The exhibition itself was
made poignant by the absence of
Maqbul Fida Husain, a member
of the original group and post-
Independence India's most flam-
boyant and controversial artist.
Now in his seventies, Husain is
famous for courting publicity,
creating instant canvases which
capture the public mood. He has

honoured cricketers, movie stars, politicians and Mother Teresa. Still painting and still controvesial, his absence was explained by the arrest warrant
issued in his name. An old sketch of his had surfaced and, alleged the city
authorities, 'threatened communal harmony'.

Three months earlier, that old sketch of a nude Saraswati, Hindu goddess
of learning, had sent convulsions across India. Neither lascivious nor deri-
sive, the sketch (*Index*, July 1997) originally stirred nothing but admiration.
But times have changed in India. A militant brand of Hinduism, *Hinduttva*,
has reared its ugly head. Protests against Husain's sketch made much of the
fact that he is nominally a Muslim. Such protests are no longer the views of
isolated extremists: the largest party in parliament is the Bharatiya Janata
Party, champions of the Hindu cause and, for 12 days in 1996, India's ruling
party.

Husain fled to the safety of London and apologized to those offended by
his sketch. Clearly it was not enough to make Bombay safe for a visit. That
October, in Ahmedabad, the city from which Mahatma Gandhi led his
famous Salt March in 1930, *Hinduttva* storm-troopers had ransacked a private art gallery due to mount a major Husain retrospective and slashed the
canvases. Had they encountered Husain, he could have met the same fate.
After all, leaders of another militant party, the Shiv Sena, the governing
party in Maharashtra state, of which Bombay is the capital, had boasted how
Muslims had been taught a lesson in early 1993, after the destruction of the
Babri Masjid in Ayodhya when riots had left at least 1,500, mainly Muslims,
dead. While the Bombay police was prompt in instituting a case against
Husain for disturbing communal harmony, the Ahmedabad police has yet to
charge anyone for destroying his paintings.

In the course of that December evening in Bombay's new art gallery, a
group of artists unfolded a banner that read: 'Husain, we miss you!' As the
night lengthened and grew chill, conversation became heated. A well known
US collector of Indian art, incensed by what had happened to Husain, asked
critics and painters present why they hadn't protested louder against the
assault on his artistic freedom. A guest replied: 'This is like asking us to speak
out in Berlin in 1936.'

Some months later, Husain, who lives and works in Bombay, returned to
the city where he was immediately called in for interrogation by the police.

Salil Tripathi, formerly a correspondent for India Today*, is now southeast Asian economic correspondent for the* Far Eastern Economic Review

AMIT CHAUDHURI

Partition as exile

The story of Partition does not stop in 1947: it is not the story of a moment but the story of exile, movement and resettlement; an agonised transition from old to new that presages the preoccupations that have come to dominate the latter half of this century

IN school in Bombay, we were taught a certain narrative about modern Indian history. Like all constructive narratives, it told a story of key moments, and thus it had an almost mnemonic quality that made it impossible to forget. Some of these key moments were, for instance, the inception of the Indian National Congress in Bombay, Gandhi's Dandi march against the salt tax, the Quit India Movement, Partition, Independence. At this point the narrative stopped, as if history had ceased to exist with Partition and Independence. But it had not ceased; it had probably become ourselves.

We, in the classroom, came to accept Partition as an event, more importantly a concept, that fundamentally defined our country's history as well as our own; this, in spite of the fact that we were living in a place, Bombay, that had little to do directly with Partition and its aftermath, and that most of the pupils in the class were Gujarati, Parsi, Maharashtrian, South Indian, whose parents came from parts of India unaffected by Partition. I was an exception, because my parents were born and grew up in East Bengal, and lost their homes and property in 1947.

Yet the historical narrative we were taught in school, with its emphasis on Partition and freedom, did not accentuate nor define, in my mind, my parents' experiences and lives, and my own place as a child of people displaced from their homeland; if anything, it suppressed such formulations. Even now, I find it hard to connect the two. Partition, as a concept taught in the classroom, as part of a narrative taught to middle class Indians as the *Mahabharat* and *Ramayan* were once disseminated in feudal Hindu India, served to define ourselves as members of this middle-class looking back upon the creation of our new nation, and suggesting, implicitly, the part we would play in totalising and interpreting it. Every time this historical narrative would be repeated by us in the future, it would be a way of once having belonged to that classroom; would restate the role we had been assigned then, as members of the middle class, as the only ones who had grasped the idea of the nation as a narrative, a totality, and our responsibility to control and interpret it.

Partition as it existed in my parents' memories, however, and in the memories of other members of my extended family, was another matter altogether; its presence seemed to be, as it were, fragmentary and poetic rather than narrative and total. Its part in my life is profound but its entire meaning still unclear. It had no fixed identity, as the Partition in the textbook did; it meant different things at different times; at times it meant nothing at all. It was disruptive rather than definitive; and it was part of a story that involved personal history, memory, family lore and vernacular; it had no overarching, decisive key role to play, but nor had its meaning ever stopped unravelling. Its relation to the Partition described in the school textbook, and described again and again even now in reports, films, and recent novels in English – many of which are fictionalised versions of the official historical narrative of India – was the relation that the semi-conscious and half-remembered have to the waking world.

Too many novels in English that have come out of metropolitan India in the 1980s and 1990s, and too much of what has been said recently during the fiftieth anniversary of Independence, have taken us back to the key historical moments we were taught about in the classroom involving the creation-myth of the nation: Partition and Independence. It is as if Indian history doesn't exist outside that fixed, unchanging, historical narrative: history, thus, risks becoming ahistorical, for history is dynamic and lived through, while the ahistorical is static and timeless. Again and again we return to the long line of refugees going towards Pakistan, and the other long line moving in the opposite direction, towards Punjab in India; one train full of corpses arriving in Pakistan, another train carrying the dead arriving in India. Independence, at the stroke of midnight, created a nation; simultaneously, Partition truncated

it; to write about India and its history we must return to the classroom
repeatedly. The rehearsal of the historical narrative becomes, then, not so
much an exploration and an enquiry into experience as, implicitly, an
exercise of power, an identification of ourselves as the rightful possessors
and interpreters of that narrative.

During the time of freedom and Partition, my father, already having
lost his homeland in Sylhet, a student in Calcutta in Scottish Church
College, was thinking of going to England. In 1947, my mother was
worrying about who would marry her, a daughter of a family without a
father, once well-to-do, but long struggling since her father's death; in
1948 she accepted my father's proposal, but no sooner had this unex-
pected stroke of good fortune occurred than she had to reconcile herself
to a prolonged engagement and the postponement of the marriage as my
father went to England as a student. The movement from Sylhet to
Shillong after the referendum and Partition, although startling, was not
wholly new to her or her family; their life had anyway been a series of
movements from one house to another since their father's death, and
then from one town to another: Sylhet, Naugang, Shillong. It might be
said that freedom and Partition, which would affect my parents' lives
profoundly, were met by them with a certain degree of incomprehension
and even indifference; for key moments, unlike their representations later
in texts, do not really have clear outlines, and might not even be perceived as having really happened; just as it is impossible to accept as real,
on a non-rational, physical, fundamental level, the absolute absence of a
loved person when that person has died. Often, one does not mourn
until much later, and then, possibly, at the provocation of some seemingly irrelevant stimulus. The human reaction to change, whether personal
or in the form of historical events, is extremely complex, a complexity, a
hiatus of the mystery or incomprehension of a response, not allowed for
in official versions of history.

Partition in Bengal is central to the film-maker Ritwik Ghatak's work
– not the movement of Partition itself, or its place and representation
in the nationalist historical narrative, but its human, almost elemental,
story of displacement and resettlement. In Ghatak (who was of East
Bengali origin, was married to an East Bengali and drank himself to
death when he was in his early fifties), Partition becomes a metaphor for
migration, resettlement and exile, among the most profound preoccupa-

tions of twentieth-century creative artists everywhere; for the twentieth century is an age of great and continuing displacement, in which the enquiry into the meaning of 'home' and 'foreignness' is continual. In this sense, Ghatak's films (the best of which were made in the 1960s), whose ostensible subject-matter mainly concerns the lives of middle-class and lower-middle-class East Bengalis, presages the literature and art of diaspora that have come to dominate the latter half of this century.

Let me dwell briefly on certain characteristic images in Ghatak's films that make his work, for me, a visionary meditation on the kind of movement and trajectory that marked the lives of my parents and others from their background. For the West Bengali, the Partition of Bengal represented an undesired truncation of the land; but, for the East Bengali, Partition signified the complete loss of the old world and the sudden, violent recreation of a new one. Ghatak's images of Partition, thus, are the elemental ones of land, water, and sky, suggesting the composition of the universe in its original form, and belonging to a mythology of creation. It's not so much history-book Partition we have here as the world as an immigrant or exile or newcomer would see it, starting from scratch and reconstructing his life and his environment from nothing. Air, water, and sky recur, the properties available to the first man and to the homeless. *Meghe Dhaka Tara* (Stars Covered by Clouds), a film about lower-middle-class East Bengali refugees struggling to start life again in Calcutta, begins with a scene in which we see only land and resettlement; the river, which is probably the Padma, separating West Bengal from what then was East Pakistan, looks more like a sea: water and horizon. The elements, configuring the process of the world in creation, recur in other films: *Titash Ekti Nadir Naam* (A River Called Titash) is dominated throughout, for instance, by images of deltas of sand emerging from the water – prehistoric images of erosion and creation, as it were – turning the film into a metaphor for the process of displacement and renewal, although its story concerns the life of a community by a river.

Subarnarekha takes as its title the name of a river never actually seen in the film. Most of the story unfolds in Ghatshila, a mining area; the protagonist, an East Bengali refugee, with his daughter, a child of six or seven, and a boy from the refugee camp whom he has adopted, arrives at a mine at which he has been appointed foreman. Later, the daughter and adopted boy will fall in love; forbidden to marry by the protagonist, they will flee to Calcutta, where they will have a child. Trauma after trauma will follow; both adopted son and daughter will die; the protagonist will return from Calcutta to the mine with his grandchild.

The backdrop against which this mainly takes place is the stark white rocks of Ghatshila; not the lush greenness associated with Gangetic Bengal, but this dream-image of prehistory, as if the rocks had just cooled and the world were new. It is through these images suggesting the original creation of the universe that Ghatak makes material the inner world of Partition, of apocalypse and rebirth. This serene background, where the historical and the natural seem to be as good as identified with each other, frames, almost indifferently, the small drama of the story's human characters. Partition, according to this vision, which conflates the natural, the geographic and the political, is seen as almost predetermined; and exile, displacement, and movement a condition of human existence.

Movement, exile and displacement, as that which occurred in my parents' lives and others of their milieu and generation, have been part of life in India from the beginning of the twentieth century, and probably before; during Partition, movement and exile simply took place on a mass scale, and with sudden and violent intensity and coercion. But the story of Partition is not the story of a moment, because it does not stop in 1947, but the story of exile, movement and resettlement, the agonised transition from old to new, and also the search for happiness in one's 'own' country that was also a 'foreign' country, India. ❏

Amit Chaudhuri was born in Calcutta in 1962 and grew up in Bombay. He is the author of two novels, A Strange and Sublime Address *and* Afternoon Raag. *A third,* Freedom Song, *is about to be published in the UK by Picador*

DAVID BERGMAN

Generation 71

THE story of impunity over the last 25 years and the political movement in Bangladesh to bring alleged war criminals to justice is rarely told.

One of Sheikh Mujibur Rahman's first political promises as leader of the new state of Bangladesh was to bring to justice those who had committed war crimes during the preceding nine month independence war, in which over one million Bengalis were killed. This genocide, perpetrated by the Pakistan army, began in March 1971, and concluded in the last few days before the surrender of the Pakistan army with an attempt to eliminate the Bengali intellectual elite.

The Bangladesh state has never been able to deliver on this pledge. Initially, international pressure coupled with Mujib's desire for 'national reconciliation' contributed to its failure. Later, the imposition of military rule (following Mujib's assassination in 1975), and the re-emergence of forces in Bangladesh which had collaborated with the Pakistan military, paralysed any possibility of accountability for war crimes.

Twenty five years on, the unsettled scores of the Liberation war continue to haunt politics in Bangladesh. One legacy of this history of impunity is the success of many alleged war criminals in acquiring positions of leadership and influence, both inside Bangladesh and within Bangladeshi communities abroad.

In 1990, with the return to democracy, demands that the state prosecute local Bengali 'collaborators' for war crimes resurfaced. This chimed with a new national mood which sought to recover the histories of the Liberation struggle. With the victory of the Awami League – Mujib's party that had led the Liberation movement – in last year's elections, after 20 years out of power, there is a real possibility that Mujib's daughter, the new prime minister of Bangladesh, will achieve what her father failed to do.

The main local collaborators of the Pakistan military were the followers of the Islamist *Jamaat-i-Islami* Party. The party's support was based in part on its total antagonism to the avowedly secular politics of the Awami League. During the war, the *Jamaat* turned its youth wing into an armed militia, *Al Badr*, which hunted down supporters of the independence movement whom it identified as enemies of Islam. The slaughter of the Bengali intellectuals in the week before the surrender of the Pakistan military was its work.

The new state of Bangladesh faced demands for war crimes trials of both the Pakistan army officers who were then held in India as well as their local collaborators who had failed to escape from Bangladesh. In the meantime, many of the leaders of the *Jamaat* and *Al Badr* had already fled the country fearing retribution. The government ban on the *Jamaat* and other fundamentalist parties had made legitimate political activity impossible. Many escaped to Pakistan, some to England, others to the USA and Canada.

The few trials that did take place in Bangladesh faced international criticism

16 December 1971, 'Victory Day' in Bangladesh: the family of Sirajudddin Hossain, editor of Ittefaque, a leading nationalist paper, murdered two days earlier in Al Badr's massacre of the intellectuals. One of his sons, Towheed Reza Noor, is now a leading member of Generation 71, an organisation of the children of those who disappeared or were victims of genocide. It campaigns to bring war criminals to justice.

for their failure to distinguish clearly between political collaboration and war crimes. In addition, two years later, Mujib issued a general amnesty for those who had committed 'political crimes'. Although this specifically excluded those involved in serious violence, in effect the whole process of accountability came to a halt.

In 1973, the government instituted new legislation in order to be able to proceed against Pakistan military officers still held in India. It allowed for war crimes trials within Bangladesh and provided the Indian government with the names of 195 officers whom Bangladesh wished to stand trial. However, by 1974, under pressure from the Indian government, which was by then seeking some sort of peace with Pakistan, and concerned about the thousands of Bangladeshis held in West Pakistan since the beginning of the war, Mujib signed an agreement that allowed the officers to return to Pakistan.

Any further moves by the Awami League were abruptly curtailed by the assassination of Mujib in August 1975. This led to 15 years of military dictatorship that depended for support on 'collaborationist' political forces. In 1977, General Ziaur Rahman, ironically, a celebrated freedom fighter in the 1971 war, allowed the *Jamaat* to return to active politics in Bangladesh; many of its members returned to Bangladesh, including its leader Golam Azam, who had lived the intervening years in Britain. In their interests, the true history of the liberation war was suppressed and distorted .

In the meantime, *Al Badr* leaders who lived abroad established sister *Jamaat* organisations in their respective countries. In Britain, for instance, at least two of the leaders of *Dawatul Islam* were senior members of the *Al Badr* accused of many killings. By the early 1980s, *Dawatul Islam* had gained total control of the biggest mosque serving the Bangladeshi community in Britain.

The impunity the *Jamaat* has enjoyed may, however, be coming to an end. With the backing of the Awami League government, the Bangladesh CID has finally launched an investigation into a number of men, all currently or previously involved in *Jamaat* politics and all living abroad, alleged to have committed war crimes. The government has, meanwhile, initiated the trial – now in progress – of the alleged murderers of Mujib. There is also growing support within the country for the trial of *Jamaat* leaders known to have been involved in the atrocities of 1971 and still resident in Bangladesh. ❑

David Bergman is a freeelance TV producer. His documentary on Bangladesh, The War Crimes File, *made with Gita Sahgal, was shown on UK TV in 1995*

From Pavlov to Pavarotti

O N the morning after Diana was buried, a Salvation Army band struck up its doleful strain of marginalised faith and blue-remembered collieries in an oval London 'square' which, in spring, looks remarkably like parted lips. Kaye came over to convey the Word but had the grace to avoid the obvious.

We spoke of other things. The minutes passed against the music's dignified lustre: strangers behaving humanly. An old woman, long-habituated to a life indoors, popped up from her basement and probed: 'Is this something to do with Di?'

It was, and it wasn't. The stoic brass, with its echoes of loss and renewal, was so apt that it might have been scripted – as had so much of our collective lives in the preceding week. Men and women could be seen groping back into the sunlight from the rubble of their private lives, eyes swollen by too much television. Some may have glimpsed their own destinies: the apotheosis of the human into an unwitting consumer of secondhand emotion, transfixed by the beams from the screens.

What happened to emotions during that week is hard to define: for the silent majority, they were snatched from the cradle before they could flourish as autonomous thought-creatures. We knew that something unimaginable was unravelling, but the half-formed reactions were bamboozled into channels not of our own making to feed a bonfire of regret, not necessarily of our own choosing.

It became clear, as the shock receded, that those who did not subscribe to this flood of grief had only excluded themselves from an 'experience'. It was an opportunity to participate in an extended mass confession; a purging of responsibility for Diana's death, which segued seamlessly – and shamelessly – into a celebration of the end of the Conservative era under which she, not we, had sparkled.

Stranger turned to stranger to dab their eyes, united into one classless, caring family by what the UK – or its media – 'does best': taking powerful mass emotions, whether over the Ethiopian famine, the World Cup or the death of a princess and transforming them into spooky spectacles of feel-good nationalism, rounded out with an aria by Pavarotti or a ballad by Elton John.

Diana's death gave an insight into where the media, at both ends of the spectrum, are ineluctably heading in the West: the Colosseum. Compare a 1997 front page with one from 10 years ago: where there were 12 stories, there are now six; where there were six, there are now three.

The Diana 'industry' owed less to her undeniable charisma, than the media owners' need to cut costs in the cannibal tabloid wars. They could no longer show a profit by covering the real news – and suspected that the public wasn't that partial to it either – so they manufactured an ersatz version eerily akin to the world of dream. With devastating effect.

For real acts of nastiness were excised from public awareness with every published shot of the princess. Every paparazzo 'snoop' prevented a genuine photo-journalist from bringing back a true portrait of the world outside the frame. Every palace denial undermined the viability of a stringer in Lagos or East Timor. Willingly or not, we had all become Diana-watchers.

Her death and the backbiting that followed concentrated 'news' into a single-issue, soap-opera requiem, with a well-thumbed cast of heroes and villains. It coincided with – and swiftly quashed – the first news from Algeria to appear on UK front pages: the slaughter of 256 civilians in Sidi Raïs.

It blurred analysis of the BBC's decision to homogenise news flow to all its radio and television programmes, including the External Service. A foretaste of that appeared on the morning after her death, when news was broadcast from a single source throughout every one of the network's stations.

Diana always warned that she had gotten 'in the way': in more ways than one.

The word on everyone's lips in the weeks after her death was privacy. Those who criticised her in life did so only discretely after death, finding a furtive consensuality in the macabre Diana joke. Walking through London's deserted streets, it was a shock to find that death had undone so many.

Media-tweaked celebrity poses as greatness; media-whipped tears only simulate grief. Within six weeks of her death, the 'right to grieve' over the 'People's Princess' had been shouldered aside by the right to know about a Conservative MP fornicating beneath a duvet.

The mother of eight children killed in the massacre of Bentalha on 23 September, whose pain was circulated around the world as a photo called the 'Algerian Pietà', would not be consoled.

She was crying for real. ❏

Michael Griffin

A censorship chronicle incorporating information from Amnesty International (AI), Article 19 (A19), the Committee to Protect Journalists (CPJ), the Canadian Committee to Protect Journalists (CCPJ), the International Federation of Journalists (IFJ/FIP), Human Rights Watch (HRW), the Media Institute of Southern Africa (MISA), the Network for the Defence of Independent Media in Africa (NDIMA), International PEN (PEN), Radio Free Europe/Radio Liberty (RFE/RL), Reporters Sans Frontières (RSF), the World Organisation Against Torture (OMCT) and other sources.

AFGHANISTAN

On 29 September, European Commissioner for Humanitarian Affairs, **Emma Bonino**, along with 18 associates including journalist **William Shawcross** and **Christiane Amanpour** of Cable News Network (CNN), were detained for nearly four hours by Taliban guards in Kabul. Four people had been filming patients at the only hospital now permitted to treat women, when a doctor alerted the authorities. Armed Taliban arrived shortly thereafter. One aid worker was assaulted during the arrest. (CPJ, *International Herald Tribune*)

In mid-October, Bangladesh's **Grameen Bank**, a pioneer of small-business loans to poor women, closed its Kabul branch. The break came after the Taliban accused the bank of being an economic wing of Christian missionary movements and of 'promoting shamelessness among Afghan women'. (*Financial Times*)

Recent Publication. *Continuing Atrocities Against Civilians* (AI, September 1997, 4pp)

ALBANIA

The parliamentary media commission, on 26 August, rejected a Democratic Party demand that one-third of news broadcasting time be given to the opposition. Commission Secretary Nikolle Lesi said the proposal would lower reporting standards by pressurising journalists to create news artificially. On 8 September Democratic Party member **Pjeter Arbnori** ended a 20-day hunger strike in protest after his party and the governing Socialists reached an agreement which allocates parties air time on the basis of the number of votes received in the 29 June election. (RFE/RL)

Socialist deputy Gafurr Mazreku shot **Azem Hajdari**, a deputy from the opposition Democratic Party, four times on 18 September. The incident took place inside the parliament building one day after the two deputies had been seen trading punches. (B92, *Albanian Media Monitor*)

ALGERIA

A director's female assistant, working for state television, had her throat cut on 31 August, when she was stopped at a bogus checkpoint. (Reuters)

Reports in September suggested that journalist **Aziz Bouabdallah**, detained at the Châteauneuf barracks by police since 11 April (*Index* 3/1997, 5/1997), was tortured to death within three days of his arrest. (RSF)

On 25 September the authorities removed the accreditation of one of the four journalists working in the Algiers bureau of **Agence France Presse** (AFP). The unnamed journalist was told that his accreditation was being rescinded because AFP had committed a 'repeat offence in his coverage of the violence. AFP, the only western news agency operating in the country, was first at the scene of the 29 August massacre at Sidi Rais, in which 256 people were reported killed. An AFP photographer, known as **Hocine**, took the image of a grieving mother after the later massacre at Bentalha which was published around the world on 26 September and became known as the 'Algerian Pieta'. Police had unsuccessfully attempted to confiscate the picture. (RSF, *Guardian*)

The human rights lawyer **Mohamed Tahri** was arrested on 20 October during a demonstration in front of Algiers' central post office by women demanding news of their missing relatives. Tahri specialises in tracing 'disappearances'. *(Le Monde)*

ARGENTINA

On 11 September four men

identifying themselves as police officers abducted **Adolfo Scilingo**, a former navy captain, and carved the letters G, M and V into his face with a knife. 'For Grondona, Magdalena and Verbitsky,' said one of the assailants, 'who are your associates'. **Mariano Grondona, Magdalena Ruiz Guinazu** and **Horacio Verbitsky** are all journalists with the Buenos Aires-based organisation Periodistas. In March 1995 Scilingo admitted to his role in throwing 30 people out of planes into the sea during the 'Dirty War'. On 8 October, he was arrested in Madrid after travelling to Spain to appear on television and to give evidence before Judge Baltasar Garzon, who is pursuing an enquiry into the disappearances of 600 Spanish immigrants during the 1976-83 period. On 13th October a high court prosecutor challenged Garzon's decision to arrest Scilingo. The attack followed President Carlos Menem's invitation to the public on 8 September to use the *ley de palo* ('the law of the stick') against members of the media who offend them. On 17 September President Menem denounced as a 'blatant lie' a *New York Times* editorial which claimed he had encouraged violence against journalists. The paper cited 800 attacks on, or threats against, journalists since Menem's term began in 1989.(Reuters, Periodistas)

Carlos Suarez, journalist, investigator and parliamentary adviser, was kidnapped at gunpoint in Buenos Aires on 21 September. Suarez was taken to a house, had a hood placed over his head and interrogated for eight hours over his enquiries into links between the administration of President Menem and the anti-Castro Miami Group organisation. Suarez is shortly to publish a book, *Globalization and the Mafia in Latin America*, which will outline the activities of the Miami Group. (Periodistas)

On 4 October **Delfo Rodriguez**, sub-director of photography for the newspaper *Los Andes*, was arrested and threatened by police while covering a football match in Mendoza. He was taken to a police station, strip-searched and held in a cell without charge for six hours. Rodriguez was harassed on the grounds that he was 'active in seeking justice in the Cabezas case' and he was threatened with the same fate. **Jose Luis Cabezas**, a photographer for the magazine *Noticias*, was murdered on 25 January (*Index* 2/1997, 3/1997, 5/1997). (Periodistas)

AZERBAIJAN

The *Forum* newspaper, which published its first edition on 12 September, was withdrawn from sale two days later and banned after one week. The minister of mass media and information, Sirus Tebrizli, blamed the *Forum*'s 'oppositional tendency'. On 18 September, the Baku newspaper *Bakinski Rabochiy* published a decree by President Heydar Aliyev which relaxes regulations limiting the reporting of military matters. Jahangir Ildrymzade, head of the republic's censorship department, said the change was aimed at 'easing the work of the media'. (RSF)

BAHRAIN

On 11 October, the State Security Court sentenced **Mohammed Yousif Abdul Wahab, Hashim Taj Hashim** and **Mahmood Ahmad Dhaif** to four years, two years and one year respectively for demanding the restoration of the dissolved parliament. (Bahrain Freedom Movement)

BELARUS

On 3 September the Soros Foundation closed its Minsk office after systematic pressure from the authorities and 'exorbitant fines'. Belarus is the only post-communist state where the foundation has suspended its programmes. (*Financial Times*)

On 4 September President Lukashenka confirmed reports that cameraman **Dimitri Zavadsky**, one of the two Russian Public Television (ORT) journalists detained since the end of July (*Index* 5/1997), had been released. He said he would order the release of Russian ORT journalist **Pavel Sheremet** once the investigation into his case had been completed. Despite President Boris Yeltsin's appeals to release both journalists prior to Lukashenka's trip to Moscow on 6 September, Sheremet

continued to be held until 8
October when he was
released, subject to him not
leaving the country.
(RFE/RL, *International Herald
Tribune*)

At the funeral of **Yevhenii
Mikolutsky** on 6 October,
Lukashenka blamed local
businessmen for the explosion
which killed the Mohilev
State Control Committee
chairman. 'If in one week,' he
said, 'commercial structures
do not hand over the names
of those who organised the
murder...his killers will face
tougher steps than anyone can
imagine.' He added: 'We will
not look for a lot of evidence
– your every
misdemeanour...will lead to
inevitable demands from our
side.'(RFE/RL)

A Minsk court fined **Pavel
Serinets** and **Yevgeniy
Skochko** US$10 each for
taking part in a demonstration
on 12 October in which an
effigy of the president was
burned. (RFE/RL)

**Waldo Albarracin
Sanchez**, president of the
Permanent Human Rights
Assembly of Bolivia, has been
the subject of long-term
harrassment and threats. He
was abducted, tortured and
left in a cell of the Technical
Judicial Police in January and
since has received death
threats at his home and at the
college attended by his
children. On 1 September he
received a telephone message
that his son had been run
over by a car. The message
proved false. (OMCT,

Reuters)

Two articles aimed at
reforming the code of
criminal procedure are
proceeding through the
legislature. Article 264 will
oblige journalists to reveal
their sources to a judge, if the
information is considered
'indispensable' to a legal
prosecution. Article 427
would give judges the power
to prevent the media from
covering certain trials. All
trials are now open to the
media. (RSF)

On 1 September some 300
Bosnian Serb civilians
surrounded and threw stones
at SFOR soldiers, who had
taken control of a television
transmitter at Udrigovo.
When NATO agreed to cede
control of the tower on 5
September, the Committee to
Protect Journalists expressed
concern regarding
opportunities for alternative
broadcasting. Republika
Srpska's Minister of
Information, Svetlana
Siljegovic, claimed the
international community had
been 'engaging in censorship'.
A deal between President
Bilijana Plavsic and her
hardline political opponent,
Momcilo Krajisnik, brokered
by Yugoslav President
Slobodan Milosevic,
temporarily defused the two
sides' battle for control of the
media when they agreed to
alternate broadcasts between
the studios at Pale and Banja
Luka. On 12 September the
US authorised the dispatch of
three EC130 aircraft to jam
radio and TV programmes

from Pale in response to
continuing ethnic propaganda
which, it maintained, had
contributed to violence in the
Bosnian Serb enclave. After
'highly provocative'
tampering with a broacast by
the UN war crimes
prosecutor **Louise Arbour**,
SFOR troops took control of
four television transmitters
under Bosnian Serb control in
the early hours of 1 October.
President Plavsic implored
NATO to respect the
agreement with her rivals
which allowed equal access to
the media. The international
community informed the
management of Bosnian Serb
Television studios in Pale it
would have to replace its
editorial staff, if it wished to
resume control of the
transmitters. Carlos
Westendorp, the international
community's chief
representative in Bosnia,
insisted on 9 October on the
dismissal of the state media
manager, **Miroslav Toholj**, in
a bid to provide audiences in
the Republic Srpska with
'access to free and
independent information'.
This was rejected by Prime
Minister Gojko Klickovic as
'unreasonable'. In an attempt
to resolve the media conflict,
Drago Vukovic was appointed
temporary general manager
for Serb radio and television.
On 13 October he claimed
TV Pale would be on the air
again by the end of the week.
(*Independent*, B92, CPJ,
RFE/RL, *International Herald
Tribune*, World Press Freedom
Committee)

Stefan Borg, a journalist
with the privately-owned
Swedish television station

TV4, was shot in the arm and back after the vehicle in which he was travelling from Sarajevo to Pale was attacked on 14 September. Four days later a Danish television crew reporting on the OSCE was atttacked on the same route as it returned from Sarajevo. (RFE/RL)

On 6 October the Serbian news agency Tanjug reported that the ministry of education in the Muslim-Croat Federation in western Bosnia had sent questionnaires to primary and high-school children in Tuzla asking if they wanted Croatian or the 'so-called Bosnian language' as the medium of tuition. A group of Muslim parents sent the ministry a strongly-worded letter which called the idea 'fascist' and a 'form of apartheid'. According to the agency, the 'act' setting up ethnically homogenous schools was signed by the Muslim minister, Fahrudin Rizvanbegovic and his Croat deputy, Jovan Pehar and was 'passed under great pressure from the Croat side, which does not recognise the language which the Muslims call Bosnian and the so-called Bosnian curricula.' (Tanjug)

On 9 October a bomb destroyed a car belonging to **Gordan Matrak**, editor-in-chief of the Banja Luka daily *Glas Srpski*. (RFE/RL)

BULGARIA

Following legislation passed in July (*Index* 5/1997), over 1,000 citizens registered on 1 September to see if secret files had been kept on them by the communist-era state security service. The Constitutional Court on 22 September rejected an appeal by 52 opposition deputies to declare the law on opening the files unconstitutional. But the court ruled that the law could jeopardise the ability of the president, vice-president and members of the court to fulfill their duties. The files of the holders of these posts will not be opened. (RFE/RL)

Ivan Stavrev, the Grand Master of the Bulgarian Lodge, announced on 22 September that freemasonry had been legalised again after a 57-year ban. (RFE/RL)

A law was approved on 9 October which strips debtors of their rights to bank secrecy, in an attempt to alleviate the country's bad loans record. On the same day, parliament passed a law allowing government departments and the state prosecutor's office to use phone tapping and other monitoring techniques, after receiving court authorisation. (RFE/RL)

BURUNDI

Prosper Nzeyimana, a journalist with national television corporation, **André Nyanawi** and **Jacqueline Segahungu**, journalists with the private radio station Umwizero, were questioned by police on 18 September after attending a press conference held by the opposition party UPRONA. The journalists' recordings of the conference were confiscated. (RSF)

CAMBODIA

The government announced a 30-day suspension of the opposition newspaper *Prayuth* on 9 September for allegedly reporting inflated casualty figures from the fighting in northern Cambodia. The information ministry is charging the newspaper with providing 'false information with the intention to incite and demoralise the Royal Cambodian Armed Forces under a law that provides criminal penalties for publications that 'affect national security or political stability.' (CPJ)

On 15 October two grenades were thrown into the compound of the newspaper *Koh Santepheap*. No one was injured. (RSF)

CANADA

On 14 October Defence Minister Arthur Eggleton introduced measures to streamline future misconduct enquiries and prevent another travesty like the investigation into the 1992-93 UN peacekeeping mission to Somalia. The action was taken in response to the final report of the Commission of Inquiry into the Deployment of Canadian Forces to Somalia (*Index* 5/1996). The commission, established in 1995 to look into allegations that troops from the Canadian Airborne Regiment (CAR) tortured and murdered Somali civilians, was cut short by the government in January before it could deal with the March 1993 murder of teenager **Shidane Arone**.

The CAR was disbanded two years ago. Eggleton said that no further charges would be brought. (Reuters, *Toronto Star*, Somalia Commission Report)

CHAD

On 25 September **Sosthene Ngargoune**, a journalist for the weekly *N'Djamena Hebdo*, was assaulted by the army officers he was interviewing at the police headquarters of the southern town Moundou. They were former members of the rebel movement Forces Armées pour la République Féderale (FARF), integrated into the army under the terms of the peace accord signed in April. They accused him and his companion, human rights activist **Dobian Assingar**, of having links with FARF. (AI)

CHILE

On 17 September the military prosecutor general presented a new petition to the Supreme Court of Justice which, if approved, would result in impunity for those responsible for human rights violations during the initial period of military government from 1973-1978. The petition calls for all appeal courts and judges to close legal proceedings into cases of human rights violations, extrajudicial executions and 'disappearances'. (AI)

CHINA

Foreign journalists were allowed access to selected meetings at the 15th

Communist Party Congress on 12 September, the first time since the 1949 revolution. A letter, supposedly written by **Zhao Ziyang**, the ousted politician who was set to be Deng Xiaping's successor, was sent to the congress demanding that the official verdict of the Tiananmen Massacre be rewritten. To call the students' movement a 'counter-revolutionary rebellion' was groundless, the letter claimed. (*Guardian, Financial Times, Independent*)

The bill to treble funding to Radio Free Asia and Voice of America, approved by a US committee on 29 September, has been criticised by the Chinese government as the 'authorising of funds for the compulsive sale of American values to China'. The new budget will increase existing services in Tibetan, Cantonese, Mandarin and to Uigur regions of Xinjiang to round-the-clock broadcasts. According to the foreign ministry, the intention of setting up Radio Free Asia was 'to use freedom of speech as a reason or excuse to interfere in the internal politics of Asian countries.' (*International Herald Tribune*)

Bishop Su Zhimin of Baoding, a prominent member of the 'underground' Catholic church, was arrested in Xinji on 8 October having spent nearly 18 months in hiding. An official at the Public Security Bureau in Hebei said there was no information on the whereabouts of Bishop Su, who has spent 20 years in

prison. The Vatican said 'two diverse sources' had confirmed his detention. (Cardinal Kung Foundation, *Catholic News Service*)

COTE D'IVOIRE

Freedom Neruda, managing editor of *La Voie* (*Index* 2/1996, 5/1996, 6/1996, 2/1997), was awarded an International Press Freedom Award from the Committee to Protect Journalists on 19 September. (CPJ)

CROATIA

Following the publication of an interview on 1 September with a former policeman who confessed to murdering Serbs during Croatia's war for independence, the editor and staff of the Split-based *Feral Tribune* were subjected to death threats. (CPJ, B92)

On 1 October the government unveiled a new penal code allowing the prosecution of journalists for reports considered 'insulting', even if they are factually correct. (Reuters)

CUBA

The director of the news agency Patria, **Ramon Alberto Cruz Lima**, was arrested at his home in Ciego de Avila on 18 August by State Security agents. Cruz had previously been arrested on 22 July in Havana, in the company of **Lazaro Lazo**, former director of the news agency Habana Press. Before being released, authorities reportedly ordered Lima to close Patria. (RSF)

CHEN FANG

Wrath of Heaven

'If you die now (said Jiao Dongfang), your reputation and integrity can be protected. When you die, any possible source for a statement about those people who are involved in your economic crimes will be gone. They'll bless your goodness in their hearts. They'll light incense for you and save your lost soul. So how about it? Are you going to take poison or shoot yourself? I've got poison and a pistol ready for you.'

...He Qizhang gave a long sigh. 'You tell Jiao Pengyuan from me, I'll be waiting for him at the gates of hell - and I'll be waiting for you too.' He Qizhang closed his eyes and made to settle his mind, trying to calm himself down. He wanted to make his death as easy as he could.

All of a sudden, he lifted his right hand with the pistol in it, the muzzle pointing dead centre between his eyebrows. His right hand was trembling a bit, and he stretched up his left to steady his right wrist, straining to point the muzzle straight at his forehead.

Jiao Dongfang stood back a little, afraid that the blood would splash him, but the muzzle of Yang Ke's pistol was aimed at He Qizhang's heart all the time.

He Qizhang pressed his back against the tree and lowered his head a little. He pulled the trigger with his right hand, and the bullet went level, coming out straight from the back of his brain. His dead body didn't fall over: it was still leaning up against the tree-trunk.

'Let's get out of here fast,' Jiao Dongfang said, 'we don't want anyone finding us out.' ❏

(translated by Jim. W)

Wrath of Heaven *(1996) was banned by the Chinese authorities in August as an over-faithful fictionalisation of the 1995 Beijing corruption scandal which led to the suicide of deputy mayor Wang Baosen and the fall from grace of Chen Xitong, the Politburo member expelled from the Communist Party during September's 15th National Congress. Chen Xiaotong, the latter's son, was sentenced to 12 years in prison in August for embezzlement. In this excerpt, 'Jiao Dongfang', son of a high-ranking party leader, pressures 'He Qizhang', deputy mayor of an*

DEMOCRATIC REPUBLIC OF CONGO

Polydor Muboyayi Mubanga, editor-in-chief of the Kinshasa daily *Le Phare*, was arrested on 8 September and nine days later charged with 'spreading false news and inciting ethnic hatred'. *Le Phare* had carried an article on 5 September reporting President Kabila's wish to create a new elite presidential guard. Kinshasa's newspapers ceased publication on 18 September in protest at Mubanga's detention. **Michael Luya**, *Le Phare*'s managing editor, was detained on 29 September. Police said that it was 'in connection with an enquiry'. (Agence France Press, Medias Libre: Medias pour Tous, RSF)

Jean-Marie Bergeziot, a French national, and **Antoine Declerc**, a Belgian, were detained and held for questioning on 10 and 16 September respectively. It is believed that the two were in possession of videotapes of alleged massacres in the Kisangani area earlier this year. (Reuters)

DENMARK

To stave off possible legislation against gangs, leaders of Hells Angels and Bandidos announced on 24 September a self-imposed ban on 'members' violence'. (*Guardian*)

EGYPT

Thomas Cromwell, editor and publisher of the *Middle East Times*, was detained by police on his arrival at Cairo airport on 22 August and put on a flight to Jordan the same day. The ministry of information has provided no explanation for his expulsion. (CPJ)

Kamal Khalil Khalil, an engineer, was detained on 29 August following his attendance at a meeting two days earlier opposing the introduction of the new land act, Law 96. Journalist **Hamdien Sabbahi**, veterinarian **Mohammad Abdu**, lawyers **Mohammad Sulayman Fayyad** and **Hamdi Haykal**, detained since 16 June for their opposition to Law 96, were released on 25 September. Student **Akram Alfy Mikha'il** and civil servant **Mostafa Mohammad Mostafa** were reportedly detained in late September for distributing leaflets criticising the lergislation. Activist **Sayyed al-Tokhi**, detained for his opposition, was released on 5 October. (Egyptian Organization for Human Rights, AI)

The twice-weekly Islamist newspaper *al-Sha'ab* was banned from publishing for three issues by the South Cairo Court on 10 September. The court had been petitioned to issue the ban by the public prosecutor as part of a criminal defamation case against six of its journalists by the Interior Minister Hassan al-Alfi. *Al-Sha'ab* circumvented the ban by printing a facsimile of its front page in the Liberal Party newspaper *al-Ahrar*. On 2 September all domestic and foreign media were prohibited from covering the case. (*Cairo Times, Le Monde*, RSF)

A freelance journalist and five employees of two Saudi-owned, London-based newspapers were convicted on 14 September of criminally libelling Ala'a and Gamal Mubarak, sons of the Egyptian president (*Index* 5/1997). The six were fined and given suspended prison sentences for producing a never-published article in the weekly *al-Jadida*. The article, which would have detailed the brothers' illegal business dealings, was given advance publicity by the daily *al-Sharq al-Awsat*. The Egyptian author of the article received a six-month jail sentence and a fine of US$4,400; the five others, who did not attend the trial, each received one-year sentences and US$5,900 fines. The judge awarded damages of £E501 (US$148) to the Mubarak brothers. This narrowly exceeds the £E500 threshold above which the brothers may seek civil damages. The paper shut its Egyptian bureau in early September. It also fired the editors who had commissioned the article. (*Cairo Times, Middle East Times*, CPJ)

A Cairo court rejected on 15 September a request to confiscate the book *Rabb al Zaman* (God of Time) by radical secularist thinker **Sayed al-Qemni**. The prosecution had been brought at the behest of the Islamic Research Academy of al-Azhar (*Index* 5/1997). Judge

Salem Salama refused to uphold any of the 19 objections raised by al-Azhar. Al-Qemni welcomed the verdict as asserting the pre-eminence of the constitution over Sharia law. Al-Azhar is seeking to have 194 other books banned. (*Cairo Times*)

The Egyptian edition of *al-Hayat* was seized on 17 September at its printers in Cairo. Censors suppressed the distribution of the Saudi-owned, London-based newspaper to prevent reporting of a visit by Sudanese President Omar Hassan Ahmad Bashir to the Halaib enclave. Egypt has disputed the area's sovereignty since Sudan gained independence in 1956. (*International Herald Tribune*)

Military prosecutors ordered a total news blackout on the 18 September petrol bombing of a Cairo bus, in which nine German tourists and the Egyptian driver died. The prosecutors have portrayed the incident as an isolated attack by two men of questionable sanity, rather than an Islamist attack. Witnesses said that the principal assailant, Saber abu al-Ulla, was helped by four others and cried '*Allahu' Akbar* as he set fire to the bus. He had previously been charged with killing three other foreigners in 1993. Abu al-Ulla told a court on 14 October that the bus attack was revenge for posters depicting the prophet Mohammed as a pig pasted on shop-fronts in Jerusalem in July by Jewish settler Tatiana Susskind (*Index* 5/1997).

(*Middle East Times, Independent, Guardian*)

On 6 October, the attorney-general barred media coverage of investigations into a high-class prostitution ring said to involve four well-known actresses. (*Middle East Times*)

EL SALVADOR

Journalist **Lorenza Saravia**, a news reader at radio station RCS in San Salvador, was 'executed' with a gunshot to the back of her head on the night of 24 August. (CPJ)

FIJI

On 3 October the senate decided to refer the *Fiji Times* to its privileges committee over an editorial, 'Practise What You Preach', which questioned the value to taxpayers of a 29 September session of an upper house meeting which lasted no more than 20 minutes. The paper, owned by Rupert Murdoch, already faces disciplinary action over revelations in December 1996 of *in camera* meetings by parliamentary sub-committees charged with reviewing the constitution. (Pacific Islands News Association)

FRANCE

Six photographers and a motorcyclist were arrested and placed under formal investigation for manslaughter on 2 September immediately after the crash which killed **Princess Diana** and **Dodi Fayed**. Reports that they had wilfully obstructed policemen

and emergency services were met with public outrage. **Romauld Rat** and **Christian Martinez** were released on bail of FF100,000 (US$16,890) each, but banned from leaving France; **Nicolas Arsov** and **Laszlo Veres** were freed without conditions; **Serge Arnal** and **Stephane Darmon** were ordered not to leave France. Rat and Martinez also had their press cards indefinitely revoked by the investigating magistrate, barring them from practising their profession. Following a protest by other photographers on 5 October, Rat had his press card returned and was told that he could resume work. Martinez had to wait a further week. Mohammed Al Fayed filed a civil suit in the case, requesting the inquiry be widened to include a violation of privacy against Dodi and Diana. Al Fayed's lawyers filed a criminal suit under the privacy laws against *Paris Match* for publishing photographs of the couple taken in St Tropez without their permission; and *Paris Match* and *France-Dimanche* for endangering the couples' lives by flying helicopters over their Riviera accommodation. (Reuters, *Guardian, International Herald Tribune, Financial Times*)

Despite a long-standing ban on sterilisations - other than those carried out for strong medical reasons - it emerged on 10 September that about 15,000 mentally handicapped women, some with only slight learning difficulties, had been forcibly sterilised without either their permission or knowledge. According to the satirical magazine *Charlie Hebdo*, this figure is a conservative one. **Nicole Diederih**, a leading academic with France's Institute for Health and Medical Research, has tried to bring the issue to the public attention since 1991. (*Daily Telegraph, International Herald Tribune*)

Brigitte Bardot was fined £1,000 on appeal in early October for inciting racial hatred in her public criticism of Muslim methods of animal slaughter. (*International Herald Tribune*)

According to a survey published on 6 October, more than three-quarters of the French reading public believe investigative journalism is unethical and that newspapers should not publish anything secret. Just over a third favoured tougher press laws. (*Guardian*)

On the eve of *Rosh Hashana*, the Jewish festivals of New Year and of atonement, the Bishop of Saint-Denis, **Msgr Olivier de Berranger**, ended a 57-year silence as he called on Jews 'to hear our words of repentance' for the Church's complicity in the wartime deaths of 73,000 French Jews. De Berranger's address, at the site of a former deportation camp north of Paris, accused wartime bishops of 'acquiescing through silence to flagrant breaches of human rights.' (*International Herald Tribune*)

President Jacques Chirac on 9

October urged 'strict imposition of the law' following the publication of a book which accuses two ex-cabinet members of ordering the 1993 killing of then opposition deputy, **Yann Piat**, who had threatened to expose 'mafia-like' activities on the Riviera. The book, by journalists **Andre Rougeot** and **Jean-Michel Verne**, blames two former ministers, known only as 'Squid' and 'Scooter' in the text, but recognisable as ex-defence minister Francois Leotard and ex-urban affairs minister, Jean-Claude Gaudin. Leotard is leader of the conservative Union for French Democracy party and is preparing to fight regional elections in 1998. (*International Herald Tribune*, Reuters)

Two journalists with the monthly *Lyon Mag*, which published the transcript of an *in camera* hearing over alleged illegal election funding by a former minister, were detained on 21 October in connection with a contempt of court enquiry. Editor **Philippe Brunet-Lecomte** and his assistant **Lionel Favrot** were held for two hours by the 'judiciary' police for refusing to reveal their source. *Lyon Mag* had published a part of the hearing in which the former mayor of Lyons and ex-minister Michel Noir admitted receiving FF1 million (US$168,900) from the construction company Bouygues to help finance the 1989 municipal elections. (Agence France Presse)

GEORGIA

Former businessman **Temur Maskhulia** told journalists on 8 October that, while under arrest earlier this year, senior security officials attempted to pressure him into giving false testimony implicating leading politicians. (RFE/RL)

GERMANY

The drug companies Willmar Schwabe, Strathmann and Bionorica, persuaded a court on 12 September to block publication of the 1997 *Drug Prescription Report* which calls on doctors to stop prescribing many medicines. The report, written by leading pharmacologists, claims that 20 percent of prescription drugs offer no real clinical benefits. **Ulrich Schwabe**, director of the Institute for Pharmacology at the University of Heidelberg and an author of the report, suspects that details of the report were leaked to the companies by someone involved in its final production stage. (*New Scientist*)

GHANA

Kwesi Biney and **Gordon George-Iroro**, correspondents for the weekly *African Observer*, its editor and publisher **Steve Mallory** and circulation manager, **Frank Awuah**, were charged with intentional libel on 15 October. The charges are in connection with an article published in the paper in September alleging corrupt practices by the Minister of Justice Yao Obed Asamoah.

(West African Journalists Association, CPJ)

GREECE

On 8 September a press release condemned the arrest of eight members of the Initiative of Citizens Against the Holding of the 2004 Olympic Games in Athens, including the journalists **Giorgios Lieros** of *Rizospastis* and **Dimitris Bolaris** of Mega Channel. (Greek Helsinki Monitor, Minority Rights Group)

Four members of the Macedonian minority party Rainbow were due to face trial on 14 October for allegedly 'having caused and incited mutual hatred among citizens' through use of the Macedonian language. The four charged with contravening Article 192 of the Greek Penal Code are **Vasilis Romas, Costas Tasopulos, Petros Vasilidis** and **Pavlos Voskopoulos**. (Greek Helsinki Monitor, Minority Rights Group)

HAITI

Yvon Chery, director of Radiotélédiffusion Cayenne was freed by a justice of the peace on 2 September following protests calling for his release. Chery said the following day that he would initiate legal proceedings against the police officers who arrested him for violation of his residence, illegal arrest and mistreatment. (AI)

INDIA

A Supreme Court judge on 7 October ruled that phone tapping violates the rights to privacy enshrined in the constitution which cannot be amended even by parliament. (*Times of India*)

Arundhati Roy won Britain's top literary prize, the Booker, on 14 October for her debut novel *The God of Small Things*, but told reporters afterwards that she may never write again. Roy's book provoked a legal suit in the state of Kerala (*Index* 4/97). 'The whole case,' she said, 'was because somebody is annoyed by the success of the book. So further success could annoy them further.' (Reuters)

INDONESIA

Demonstrators at a march organised by the Youth Front for Upholding People's Rights in Bogor were arrested on 17 August. They were calling for freedom of speech and opinion and carried posters of the journalist **Fuad Muhammed Syarfuddin** from the daily *Bernas* who was murdered in 1996, reportedly due to his enquiries into illegal land deals (*Index* 5/1996). The organisation's headquarters was raided on 19 August. (HRW)

Two Jakarta-based Dutch journalists were arrested and film from a CNN camera crew was seized at the annual meeting of an unrecognised labour union on 19 September. The leader of the Indonesian Labour Welfare Union has been in detention for over a year on subversion charges. (Institute for the Studies on Free Flow of Information)

Plantation companies and ministers continue to insist that the fire and smoke which engulfed south east Asia in mid-September were caused by the prolonged drought. Illegal logging was under investigation by freelance journalist **Naimullah**, who was killed on 25 July. (*Independent*, AI)

IRAN

On 11 September, Foreign Minister Kamal Kharrazi objected to German Foreign Minister Klaus Kinkel's expression of concern at the fate of jailed Iranian newspaper editor **Faraj Sarkoohi** one day earlier (*Index* 6/1996, 1/1997, 2/1997, 3/1997, 4/1997, 5/1997). On 18 September Sarkoohi was convicted of 'malicious propaganda' and sentenced to a year in jail. In a message to his wife in Berlin, Sarkoohi said that he would probably be released in January 1998, because of time already spent in jail. (Reuters, *Guardian*)

On 11 September the government repealed a ban against the weekly *Aftabgardan* (Sunflower), a children's magazine published by Tehran's mayor **Gholamhossein Karbaschi**. Deputy Minister of Culture and Islamic Guidance, Ahmad Bourqani said *Aftabgarden* could resume publication while it appealed against a May ruling by a special press

• •

HAKIM HAQNAZAR

This sentence condemns you

THE sentence against Faraj Sarkoohi is a sentence which condemns the Islamic Republic of Iran's judicial system. It acquits Sarkoohi from the accusations made against him, but disgraces the judicial system of the republic. God will punish this ignorant tribe for they are signing their own condemnation with their own hands.

None of the offences with which they charged Sarkoohi are mentioned in the sentence. Sarkoohi was accused of the same offences for which Sa'idi Sirjani was arrested and destroyed four years ago. These ranged from spying for foreigners to opposing the revolution and Islam and having unlawful sexual relations. Each could, on the basis of the republic's laws, lead to a death sentence. Why did they not ? Because there is no justice; there is no law.

The judicial system is a tool in the hands of government, an instrument subordinate to the politics of the day. If the policy which was dominant at the time of Sa'idi Sirjani's arrest, imprisonment and death had not undergone some change in these past few months - forcing the clerical government to watch its step - then Sarkoohi's fate would have been no better than Sirjani's.

Remember how they arrested Sarkoohi. He was about to travel to Germany, like any ordinary traveller, when he disappeared into thin air. That was when the judge in the Mykonos trial, over the murder of Iranian Kurdish dissidents in Germany, had issued a verdict implicating high-ranking leaders in the Islamic republic. The regime turned around like a wounded animal to vent its venom. The choice fell on Sarkoohi. The scenario for kidnapping and getting rid of Sarkoohi was the same used by Col Mu'ammar al-Qadhafi on the Lebanese Shi'a clergyman Imam Musa Sadr in 1978.

The plan backfired because the Germans had their wits about them and were monitoring the traffic of Iranian passengers. When it was said that Sarkoohi had gone to Germany and had disappeared, Bonn brought pressure to bear and called for serious investigations into the case. The government then had to rewrite the scenario. They paraded Faraj at Mehrabad Airport as someone who had first gone to

• •

• •

Germany and then turned up in Turkistan, returning illegally on a forged passport. In trying to whitewash their mistake, they committed a bigger one. From then on, the Sarkoohi case acquired another dimension. It became clear that they intended to sacrifice this writer to settle a score with Germany and the EC.

If, after all palaver and fury, they suddenly announce that Sarkoohi has been sentenced to one year's imprisonment - which includes the time he has spent in detention - and that they even allowed him to phone his wife to tell her, it is because the policy has changed.

They say that he has accepted the court's verdict and not asked for an appeal. Any wise person would have done the same. In a country where the judicial system has meaning, one stands up and cries out one's innocence.

Since this verdict is not been based on law, it cannot be lawfully amended. It is a political verdict and it is still not clear how long the policy which required this verdict will last. Reason dictates that Faraj should save himself from the clutches of his torturers. A reversal of the present situation could see an appeal court annulling the verdict and issuing instead a death sentence against him.

If Sarkoohi's judges had wanted to do President Khatami and his new government a good turn, they should have issued a decisive verdict, erased his file and condemned the way in which he was prosecuted and harried. They should have acquitted the man and apologised. Khatami could then have said that here was one of the miraculous fruits of the 22 million votes he won in the May elections and a milestone of major changes in the ruling system.

This half-baked ruling is a testament to the half-baked nature of the current changes. As an expedient, the judiciary has been instructed to wind up the Sarkoohi case so that Germany shuts up and the EU is reconciled. But this has hardly increased the political 'space' within the country. No more jails; no more chains!

In the eyes of people like Sarkoohi, a judicial system which is the tool of the establishment and the centre of conspiracies had better not exist at all. Its existence is infinitely more harmful than beneficial even if, on this rare occasion, it has saved a man from death after a show trial. ❏

An edited version of an article in the English-language weekly Kayhan *(Universe), published in London.*

• •

court which found it guilty of violating press laws. The court ordered Karbaschi to pay a fine of some US$6,700 for publishing a satirical article which accused state radio and television of lack of impartiality in the country's presidential elections on 23 May. Karbaschi, who also heads a mass-circulation daily, actively campaigned for the moderate candidate Mohammad Khatami, who won the presidential election by a landslide. (Reuter)

'Formation of political parties is not considered unhealthy,' said the English-language *Iran News* in an editorial on 16 September, adding: 'It is now the duty and responsibilty of politicians to fill the gap and form political parties with healthy foundations and make them a model for others.' (Reuter)

Tehran newspapers said on 16 September that 'depraved' dolls were sold openly in northwestern Iran after being smuggled from neighbouring Azerbaijan. The battery-operated, *lambada*-dancing dolls, were trading at 30,000 rials (US$10), reports said. In an apparent move to compete with the widely-popular Barbie and Ken dolls, made by US company **Mattel**, the government has launched two 'traditional' dolls called Dara and Sara. (Reuters)

IRELAND

The Irish Independent Television and Radio Commission decided at the end of September that the 1970 Eurovision song contest

winner **Dana**, who is running for president, must have her air-time regulated. Whenever her hit song, 'All Kinds of Everything', is played on the radio, stations will be obliged by law to cut back, proportionately, on any coverage of her election campaign. (*Guardian*)

ISRAEL

Hossam Abu Alan, a Hebron-based Palestinian photographer working for Agence France Presse, was detained for five days after he was stopped at an army control point between Hebron and Jerusalem. He had photographed a tank. (RSF)

Recent publication: *Prisoners of Peace - Administrative Detention During the Oslo Process* (B'Tselem, July 1997, 100pp)

ITALY

At a concert in Bologna to celebrate the 23rd Italian National Eucharistic Congress, the Pope responded to **Bob Dylan**'s performance of 'Blowin' in the Wind' by censoring possible answers to its famous rhetorical question: 'How many roads must a man walk down?' The pontiff said: 'Man has just one road to travel and that is Christ.' Singer Gianni Morandi followed with a duet version of **John Lennon**'s 'Imagine', in which all references to 'no heaven' and 'no religion' were removed. (*Independent*)

Father Tissa Balasuriya, the Sri Lankan theologian

excommunicated by the Vatican in January for heresy, was denied a visa to visit Italy on 2 October. (*Guardian*)

JAPAN

On 29 August the Supreme Court ruled as illegal the deletion from school textbooks of references to Unit 731, a camp where germ experiments were carried out on live prisoners in China during World War II. The other claims against textbook screening brought by **Professor Saburo Ienaga** against the ministry of education, were thrown out of court. (*Guardian, International Herald Tribune*)

JORDAN

On 24 and 25 September the ministry of information ordered 12 weekly newspapers to close because they had failed to meet the requirements of the amendments to the Press and Publications Law, introduced on 17 May. Among the newspapers affected are: *al-Majd, al-Mithaq, al-Hadath, al-Bilad, Sawt al-Maraa, al-Sayad, Hawadeth al-Sa'a, al-Hadif, al-Faris, Tareeq al-Mustaqbal, al-Umma* and *al-Urdun*. The newspapers failed to raise their capital from US$20,000 to US$400,000. The papers have three months to raise the money or face permanent closure. (CPJ)

Ali Sneid, a 25-year-old writer, was detained by police on 26 September in connection with an article critical of a local politician. The article took a local leader to task for disparaging remarks about independent politicians in a speech made in the presence of King Hussein which was broadcast on television. Newspapers turned down the article, so Sneid made copies which he had planned to distribute. He was held incommunicado for a week before his transfer to Jwaideh prison. Sneid was detained for several days in November 1996 after he wrote a play about the trial of **Laith Shubeilat,** the president of the Jordanian Engineers Association (*Index* 3/1996, 1/1997). (HRW)

KENYA

Youths led by Daniel Kongo, an official with the ruling Kenya African National Union (KANU) party, stormed the offices of the *Sunday Standard* on 6 September, threatening to burn the offices and lynch journalists, after a story appeared in its sister paper, the *East African Standard,* which reported heckling and a no-confidence vote in Kongo at a KANU meeting the previous day. (NDIMA)

Joe Kariuki, publisher of the *Rift Valley Times* and the *Times* newspapers, and freelance journalist **Palazh Krishnanunni Raja** were arrested on 28 September after publishing a story speculating on presidential aide Joseph Kulei's personal fortune. Kariuki and **Joseph Agola,** director of the newspapers' printer Techno Press, who was arrested on 30 September, were charged with defamation on 2 October and

released on bail pending a hearing on 10 December. Raja, an Indian national and the author of the article, was charged on 3 October with being in the country illegally and working as a journalist without a permit. (NDIMA)

Vitalis Musebe, head of news at Kenya Television Network (KTN), and his deputy **Isaiya Kabira** (*Index* 5/1997), resumed work on 1 October after a three-month suspension. They were reinstated unconditionally. (NDIMA)

Recent publication: *Violations of Human Rights* (AI, September 1997, 54pp)

KYRGYZSTAN

On 2 September, the government newspaper *Nasha Gazeta* published resolution 320, concerning new customs regulations. The resolution provides for the banning of books, printed materials, films, film negatives, audio and video material, records, tapes, disks, hand-written material and data media imported into the country which 'may damage the political and economic interests, national security, public order, health protection and public morals' of the Republic. (RSF)

Ryspek Omurzakov, a journalist with the opposition weekly *Res Publika,* was found guilty of libel and sentenced to three years in a prison colony on 29 September for libelling Mikhail Paryshkura, director of the state-owned Frunze machine-building

factory in an article on 14 January 1997 (*Index* 5/1996, 2/1997, 3/1997). Omurzakov based his story on a petition about poor living quarters signed by over 100 workers. The verdict qualifies Kyrgyzstan as the first of the former Soviet republics and satellite states to have sent a journalist to prison for libel. (RFE/RL, Bureau on Human Rights and Rule of Law, CPJ)

On 28 September the 14-year-old son of **Zamira Sydykova** (*Index* 5/1995, 6/1995, 1/1997, 2/1997, 4/1997, 5/1997), chief editor of the weekly *Res Publika,* was severely beaten by members of the paramilitary police or OMON. The boy, now in hospital, was found hiding by OMON during an evening raid in Bishkek. Sydykova, a candidate for the upper chamber of parliament, said her son had not hidden because of any criminal misdemeanour, but because he was afraid. (Bureau on Human Rights and Rule of Law)

The MP **Dooronbek Sadybayev** received an official warning from Galina Pugatcheva, deputy general prosecutor, on 29 September saying that he may be charged with calling for the overthrow of the government after a series of interviews in July and August. Sadybayev had criticised presidential policy in the Kyrgyz language newspapers *Asaba, Kyrgyz Rukhu* and *Ordo.* He rejected Pugatcheva's warning on the grounds that his status as an MP protected him against prosecution and that she could not have understood the interviews, because she is not a Kyrgyz-speaker. (Bureau on Human Rights and Rule of Law)

On 29 September, Kanybek Imanaliyev, spokesman for President Akayev, told a press conference that eight lawsuits will be lodged by top officials against *Asaba* in connection with the 26 September issue. He said that eight stories in the newspaper contained slander, libel or premeditated false information directed against the president, his family, his closest advisors and aides. Imanaliyev used to be a journalist for *Asaba*. On 3 October, the pro-government dailies *Slovo Kyrgyzstana* and *Nasha Gazeta* published a statement by the presidential press-service saying that the 26 September issue 'overflowed with the dirty currents of lies, aggressiveness, slander, ... and are compromising the activities of the unanimously-elected President of the Kyrgyz Republic.' (RFE/RL, Bureau on Human Rights and Rule of Law)

Rayissa Gorbatcheva, a poet, editor and journalist, was found strangled in her apartment in Bishkek on 6 October. Her son Dennis, who discovered the body, said that an acquaintance recently released from a prison colony might be responsible. (Bureau on Human Rights and Rule of Law)

In an early-October interview with the *Slovo Kyrgyzstana,* Tursunbai Bakir-uulu, a parliamentary deputy, said he

would sue all media that had ever slandered him in print. He and his lawyers, he said, were studying every published reference since his original nomination as a candidate in 1994. Bakir-uulu was recently appointed head of the assembly's Committee on I n t e r n a t i o n a l, Interparliamentary Relations and Mass Media. (Bureau on Human Rights and Rule of Law)

LESOTHO

A ban preventing journalists from covering debates in the lower house was imposed on 28 August, after a feud erupted between the ruling Basotoland Congress Party (BCP) and the breakaway Lesotho Congress for Democracy (LCP). The speaker, Dr Teboho Kolane, lifted it on 15 September after pressure from local and international journalists. (MISA)

MACEDONIA

Rufi Osmani, the ethnic Albanian mayor of Gostivar, was sentenced to 13 years and eight months in jail for 'fanning national, racial, and ethnic intolerance, inciting rebellion and disregarding the Constitutional Court,' but was freed on 9 October. Gostivar council chairman **Refik Dauti** was also sentenced to three years in jail. Osmani and Dauti had allowed Albanian and Turkish flags to fly from the town hall during demonstrations on 9 July (*Index* 4/1995). (RFE/RL, B92, Greek Helsinki Monoitor)

MALAWI

Deguzman Kaminjolo, cartoonist and reporter for the privately-owned *Independent* newspaper, was assaulted by the Minister of Energy and Mining, Dumbo Lemani, while attending a function in Blantyre on 21 August. The minister grabbed Kaminjolo by the neck and ordered him to stop producing 'trash' about President Muluzi and the ruling United Democratic Front. (MISA)

MacDonald Mukorongo, a senior assistant air traffic controller, was interdicted on 11 September, for writing an article in the *Nation* newspaper exposing poor safety standards at the country's international airports. Mukorongo was interdicted under the 1966 Malawi Public Service Regulations Act, which prohibits civil servants from publishing or leaking information to the media. (MISA)

MALAYSIA

The Kuala Lumpur bureau chief for the *Far Eastern Economic Review* was sentenced on 4 September to three months in prison and the confiscation of his passport for contempt of court in an article written for the 23 January issue which examined details of a civil suit brought by the wife of an appeals court judge. In his article, the veteran Canadian reporter **Murray Hiebert** asserted that Datin Chandra

Sri Ram's suit against the International School for dropping her son from his school debating team had moved unexpectedly swiftly through the court system. His request for the return of his passport was refused on 3 October pending an appeal of his conviction. (RSF, CCPJ, *Guardian*)

MAURITANIA

The 2 September issue of the weekly *L'Eveil Hebdo* was banned, apparently because of an editorial titled 'It isn't de Gaulle asking' which criticised the sums the government was spending on a state visit by French President Jacques Chirac on 5-6 September. Reporters sans Frontières placed inserts criticising the state of press freedom in the weeklies *Mauritanie Nouvelles*, *Le Calame*, *L'Eveil Hebdo* and *La Tribune* during the visit. On 5 September, 14 journalists were barred from a joint press conference by Chirac and President Maaouya Ould Sidi Ahmed Taya. **Bah Ould Saleck**, editor-in-chief of *Mauritanie Nouvelles* and one of those expelled, chose not to cover Chirac's state visit in protest. (RSF)

On 2 October, the interior ministry seized copies of the French edition of *Mauritanie Nouvelles*, announcing later in the day that both French and Arabic editions were banned from publishing for three months (*Index* 3/1996, 5/1996, 4/1997). The period covers the upcoming presidential elections. The director of political affairs and public liberties, Mohamed Yeslem Ould Amar Chein, said the newspaper had been barred for reporting the formation of an 'Arab-African Front'. (IFJ/FIP, World Association of Newspapers)

MAURITIUS

Gilbert Bablee, a journalist with the weekly *Defi-Plus*, was detained on 24 September after businessman Virendra Ramdhun, whom he was interviewing, accused him of having stolen documents from his office. Bablee was trying to verify the contents of papers querying Ramdun's financial competence, which he had received through the post. He was released the same day after questioning, but the papers were confiscated. (IFJ/FIP)

MEXICO

Daniel Lizarraga, a journalist with the daily *Reforma*, was kidnapped on 5 September, beaten and interrogated for three hours by two men about his reports on police involvement in drug trafficking. On 25 August his colleague at *Reforma*, journalist **David Viventeno** was kidnapped by men whom he believes were judicial police. Viventeno had been investigating the disappearance of Jorge Francisco Palacios Hernandez, who apparently bore a striking resemblance to Amado Carrillo Fuentes, a drug trafficker who is reported to have died while undergoing plastic surgery earlier in the summer. (RSF)

On 13 September **Rene Solorio, Gerardo Segura** and **Ernesto Madrid**, journalists with TV Azteca, were abducted, assaulted and threatened with death by men who, they said, were police officers. It was not an act of aggression, they were told, but one of 'vengeance' for information broadcast by the station. The journalists had been investigating instances of corruption and human rights violations involving judicial police officers in Mexico City. (RSF)

On 17 September **Silvia Otero**, a reporter with the daily newspaper *El Universal*, was kicked and beaten as she entered the Reclusorio Oriente (Eastern Prison) in Mexico City. Otero had been investigating allegations that police officers had executed three suspected criminals in the Buenos Aires district of Mexico City. (AI)

MOROCCO

Photographer **Ahmed Laraki**, from the opposition newspaper, *al Ittihad al Ichtiraki*, was arrested along with four National Bank Union members at a 5 September demonstration calling for union recognition and negotiations with the government. All five were released later in the day. (RSF)

NAMIBIA

Parliament moved a motion on 8 September to give it powers to subpoena and demand sources of information from members of the public, including journalists. Under the Parliamentary Powers, Privileges and Immunities Act of 1996, it is already illegal to interview MPs on matters of public interest before they are tabled in the house. (MISA)

NIGER

On 7 October **Moussa Tchangari**, managing editor of the weekly *Alternative*, was sentenced to three months in prison and fined CFA50,000 (US$100) for 'publishing an administrative document intended for internal use,' which is forbidden under the 25 July press law (*Index* 4/1997). The document was a copy of a letter sent by Prime Minister Cisse Djakon to Sanoussi Djakon, minister responsible for universities, and which named two businessmen who could be awarded a CFA300 million (US$60,000) contract to supply equipment to the University of Niamey without having to go through the process of public tender. Tchangari has lodged an appeal. (RSF)

NIGERIA

On 30 August, security officers barred guests from attending the launch in Lagos of a book on Chief Moshood Abiola, the detained winner of the annulled 1993 presidential elections, by journalist **Richard Akinnola**. (International Journalism Centre)

Oby Eke Agbai, a regional leader of the Nigeria Union

of Journalists (NUJ), disappeared after her discharge from hospital where she had been treated for injuries sustained from a beating by security officers at government offices in Owerri on 3 September. (Independent Journalism Centre)

Akpandem James, a correspondent for *Punch*, was detained on 4 September for 'exaggerating' allegations by the Movement for the Survival of the Ogoni People (MOSOP) that copies of the late **Ken Saro-Wiwa**'s books were confiscated from a bookseller in Port Harcourt, Rivers state. **Chris Ikwunze**, a correspondent for *The Vanguard*, was arrested the following day in connection with the same story. Both were released on 9 September. (Independent Journalism Centre)

Dagogo Clinton, acting editor of the government-owned *Tide* newspaper in Rivers state, was suspended on 5 September in connection with an editorial lamenting the condition of the roads in Port Harcourt. (Independent Journalism Centre)

Ariet Igiebor, wife of *Tell* magazine's editor-in-chief **Nosa Igiebor**, was detained at gunpoint on the night of 10 September. Security officers had come to arrest her husband for publishing an article alleging that President Abacha suffered from cirrhosis of the liver. (Independent Journalism Centre, CPJ)

The editor of the weekly *Sunday Magazine*, **Christine Anyanwu**, who was imprisoned in July 1995 for exposing a government round-up of political opponents (*Index* 3/1995), was awarded an International Press Freedom award by the Committee to Protect Journalists on 19 September. (CPJ)

Plainclothes officers detained **Babatunji Wusu**, an administrator with the independent magazine the *News*, on 17 September for four days. They had been instructed to arrest the editors for publishing a story about international pressure on President Abacha's regime. In a related incident, two vendors in Abuja were detained on 22 September after security agents raided their stalls and confiscated all copies of the *News*. Newspaper stalls throughout the city were targeted again on 23 and 24 September to ensure that no fresh copies were on sale. **Bayo Onanuga**, editor-in-chief of the *News*, and all associated editors went into hiding after police sent a warrant for Onanuga's arrest on 3 October. The *News* and its sister titles, *Tempo* and *PM News*, continue to be published. (Independent Journalism Centre)

Reth Ateloye, librarian at the magazine *Fame*, was detained in Lagos on 17 September for reasons unknown. He was released on 22 September from a military hospital to which he had been moved after falling seriously ill, allegedly after being tortured. He died on 5 October. (Independent Journalism Centre)

On 6 October, eight journalists of Yobe State Television (YTV) were severely beaten on the orders of the state military administrator, John Ben Kalio, after airing a 45-minute documentary on the achievements of his precedessor, Dabo Aliyu. (Independent Journalism Centre)

Recent publication: *No Significant Change - Human Rights Violations Continue* (AI, September 1997, 30pp)

PAKISTAN

On 4 September the Larkana office of the Sindhi-language daily *Kawish* was ransacked by armed individuals who took away the newpaper's computers and communication equipment. It is believed that *Kawish* was targeted because it has given extensive coverage to a 3 August attack on *Awami Awaz* reporter **Shakeel Naich** by members of the Sindh National Front (*Index* 5/97). Minister of Information Mushahid Hussain Syed gave assurances that the government would take every step to protect journalists from physical assaults. On 15 September several people were injured when police charged a 300-strong procession of journalists and media workers protesting against the two incidents. (Pakistan Press Foundation)

According to a news report on 4 September, author **Muneer Ahmed** argues in his new Urdu-language book, *Will Pakistan Break Up?*, that the Inter-Services Intelligence (ISI) was responsible for the series of bomb blasts in Bombay which killed at least 228 people in March 1993. (INDOlink)

On 9 September **Humayun Fur**, the Peshawar bureau chief of the Urdu-language daily *Mashriq*, was sentenced to five years' hard labour by a military court for spying. Military intelligence arrested Fur on 28 June and the defence ministry said investigations had proved that he had passed 'sensitive state secrets' to personnel at foreign diplomatic missions in Islamabad. Fur's trial, which lasted for 27 days, marked only the second time that a journalist has been court martialled. On 2 October, Fur was transferred from Adiyala jail to hospital in critical condition and he was released on 7 October after his wife successfully petitioned the Chief of the Army Staff, General Jehangir Karamat. (*Dawn*, Pakistan Press Foundation, Reuters)

Nine photographers for the national dailies *Pakistan Observer, Khabrain, Business Times, Jang* and *Assas* were beaten up by staff at Rawalpindi General Hospital on 11 September. The photographers were attempting to take pictures of a slain worker of the religious party *Tehrik Nifas-i-Fiqh-i-Jaffaria* when they were attacked. (Pakistan Press

Foundation)

The Inter-Provincial Coordination Committee postponed the census for the fourth time on 4 October. The last census took place in 1981. Analysts believe that the urban population in Punjab, Sindh, North West Frontier Province and Baluchistan has far outstripped that in the rural areas and that the Sindh population has risen faster than that of the Punjab. If proven, such projections would upset the current power balance, which favours the traditional land-owning elite in Punjab. Article 51 of the constitution states that the number of seats in parliament must be directly proportionate to demographic trends. (*Dawn*, Muttahida Quami Movement)

Recent Publications: *Legalizing the Impermissible: The New Anti-terrorism Law* (AI, October 1997, 22pp)

PALESTINE (AUTONOMOUS AREAS)

The High Court of Justice heard on 6 September that education professor **Fatih Ahmed Subuh** was subjected to severe torture following his detention on 2 July for setting exam questions which invited students to comment on corruption (*Index* 5/1997). The allegations were not contested by the attorney-general, but the court did not ask to examine Subuh and it deferred a decision until 6 October. (AI)

On 19 September Israeli

Defence Forces prevented **Nasser Shiyoukhi**, a Palestinian reporter for the Associated Press, from entering a Jewish enclave in Hebron. A soldier told Shiyoukhi he was barred because he was an Arab. When Shiyoukhi tried to show his press card, the soldier knocked him to the ground. Israeli border guards who witnessed the incident convinced Shiyoukhi to file a complaint. (CPJ)

Palestinian police closed the Afaq television station in the West Bank on 25 September as part of their attempt to crack down on organisations supporting Hamas. The station's owner, **Issa Abu Aliz**, was detained. Police also closed 16 welfare organisations, including day-care centres, orphanages and vocational training groups, which they allege have connections to Hamas. (Palestinian Society for the Protection of Human Rights and the Environment)

Recent publication: *Palestinian Self-Rule Areas - Human Rights under the Palestinian Authority* (HRW Middle East, September 1997, 56pp)

PANAMA

On 19 September, the government served prize-winning investigative journalist **Gustavo Gorriti**, an associate editor with the daily newspaper *La Prensa*, with deportation papers after he was refused an extension on his one-year work permit (*Index* 5/1997). (*Guardian, International Herald Tribune*)

PERU

Two journalists from the magazine *Si* were found guilty of defaming media owner **Baruch Ivcher Bronstein** and given one-year suspended prison terms by a criminal court in Lima on 24 August. Bronstein, former owner of the TV station Canal 2 has been the victim of a government campaign to strip him of his interests and nationality since April when he aired allegations of torture by army intelligence agents (*Index* 3/1997, 4/97, 5/97). On 26 May, the pro-government *Si* had published a report maintaining that Ivcher had sold arms to the Ecuadorian army. Journalist **Jaime Enrique Aguilar Escobar** and *Si's* director **Juan Gullo Omodeo** were ordered to pay damages of around US$1,100. (*International Herald Tribune*, RSF)

On 31 August the body of **Tito Pilco Mori**, director of Radio Frecuencia Popular, was found. He had died from injuries to the head and chest. The circumstances surrounding his death are unknown, but a few days before he died, four individuals said they were going 'to shut him up'. (RSF)

On 19 September Associated Press (AP) photographer **Ricardo Choy** had six rolls of film seized by police at the request of Samuel and Mendel Winter, who were recently granted control of Baruch Ivcher Bronstein's Frecuencia Latina/Canal 2 television station (*Index*

4/1997, 5/1997). Choy was taking pictures of the Winters entering the Canal 2 building. After complaints by AP and several days' delay, police returned the films developed. (*Guardian*)

On 29 September, President Alberto Fujimori announced that the government would not seek renewal of 'faceless' courts when their annual life expired on 15 October. Human rights groups have condemned the courts, which operate with judges masked, or hidden behind screens. Fujimori admitted there had been 'errors', 'exaggerations' and 'anti-constitutional' acts during the four-year period of their use. As many as 1,000 individuals may have been falsely imprisoned. (AI, Reuters, *International Herald Tribune*)

ROMANIA

On 1 October the National Peasant Party Christian Democratic's (PNTCD) Disciplinary Commission suspended Senator **Ticu Dumitrescu**'s membership for one year after he repeatedly criticised the leadership's lethargy in drafting a law to open the Communist era secret police files. (RFE/RL)

RUSSIA

In accordance with a new law on freedom of conscience and religious organisations adopted by the Duma on 19 September, the authorities revoked the registration of the **Evangelical Lutheran Mission of Khakassia**

(*Index* 4/1997, 5/1997). The mission was first registered in June 1996, although its director **Rev Pavel Zayakin** later claimed that it had existed in Russia for more than 400 years. The group is to appeal. Further underlining the law's implications for small religious organisations, 'scores of leather jacketed officers, armed with semi-automatic weapons and rubber batons' attacked the **Ukrainian Orthodox** cathedral in Noginsk in a late night raid on 20 September. The archbishop was led away in handcuffs. (RFE/RL, *Independent*)

It was reported on 1 October that **Anatolii Naumov** is being held in solitary confinement awaiting extradition to Azerbaijan on charges of extortion. Currently a member of the editorial staff at St Petersburg-based *Chas Pik*, Naumov had worked as deputy editor of a Russian-language newspaper in Baku. (RFE)

On 1 October Deputy Prime Minister Boris Nemtsov accused the Russian media of a lack of objectivity and suggested that most people in Nizhnii Novogorod preferred to receive news from RFE/RL and Radio Mayak. His singling out of Russian Public Television (ORT) was seen as a veiled attack against Security Council Deputy Secretary, Boris Berezovskii, a highly influential figure in the organisation (*Index* 5/1997). Nemtsov called for greater state control over the finances and 'ideological foundations' of the network. (RFE/RL)

RWANDA

In the week beginning 3 October, **Hassan Ngeze**, former editor-in-chief of *Kangura* newspaper, was indicted to appear before the International Criminal Tribunal for Rwanda (ICTR) to answer allegations that he knowingly allowed and directed articles that incited people to participate in the 1994 genocide against the Tutsis. **Georges Ruggiu**, a former journalist with the extremist Radio Television Libre des Mille Collines, was arrested two weeks later and faces two counts of genocide and crimes against humanity. (International Criminal Tribunal for Rwanda)

Recent publications: *Burying the Truth in the Name of 'Human Rights': Antoine Sibomana and His Supporters* (African Rights, September 1997, pp88); *Ending the Silence* (AI, September 1997, 55pp)

SAMOA

Two journalists from the independent *Samoa Observer*, publisher **Savea Sano Malifa** and Samoan-language editor **Fuimaono Tupua**, were ordered to pay the costs of Prime Minister Tofilau Eti Alesana's suit for criminal libel at a hearing on 11 September (*Index* 4/1997, 5/1997). The magistrate agreed to an adjournment to allow the defendants time to bring in a New Zealand lawyer experienced in handling libel cases. A new trial date was set for 17 November. (Pacific Islands News Association)

SERBIA-MONTENEGRO

The Montenegrin government and opposition parties agreed to a pact on 1 September guaranteeing all parties equal access to the state-run media in the run-up to elections in May 1998. (RFE/RL)

On 4 September, the presidential candidate **Vojislav Seselj** claimed he had difficulty accessing some local Serb media, especially in Kosovo. The Democratic Party claimed on the same day that the Serbian information ministry had recommended local media not allow those parties boycotting the election to air any pre-election advertising. On 9 September the Democratic Party leader and mayor of Belgrade, Zoran Djindjic, claimed that fair elections would not be possible in Serbia as the opposition had no access to the state media. (B92)

On 12 September **Baton Haixhu**, associate chief editor of the Pristina daily *Koha Ditore* was interrogated for two hours about meetings with foreign diplomats, politicians and students. On the same day, two men in civilian clothing confiscated the camera of reporter **Fisnak Abrassi** as he photographed Serbian Socialist Party members visiting Pristina. On 25 September Haixhu was arrested for a second time. He was released after being questioned about planned student protests demanding equal language rights and normalisation of the province's ethnically-divided education system. The officers also took documents pertaining to two other editors, **Yiber Hysa** and **Dukagjin Gorani**. (RSF)

Bujko correspondent **Rrahim Sadiku** was halted and ill-treated at the Serbian police checkpoint of Gërlicë village near Ferizaj. He was ordered to report back to the police station on 16 September when he was again ill-treated and told he would be summoned for further questioning. (*News from Republic of Kosovo*)

Having ousted **Zoran Djindjic** as Belgrade's Democratic Party mayor, the Serbian Renewal Movement, Serbian Radicals and Socialists joined forces on 30 September to rid Studio B, the city's council-owned television station, of its editorial management. The board of directors was replaced by members from the parties involved in the action, thereby excluding the Democratic Party. The following day the remaining staff walked out in protest. A mass protest demonstration on 1 October was attacked by Serbian riot police who beat and detained a number of participants. **Dragotin Rokvic**, general secretary of the Independent Union of Journalists of Serbia, and several of his colleagues were attacked, questioned and told they would face criminal charges for allegedly throwing stones and insulting officers. (B92, CPJ, IFJ/IFP)

Protesters at student demonstrations held on 1 October in Pristina, Kosovo, were dispersed by Serbian police using clubs and tear gas. A number of the alleged organisers were detained, including the self-styled 'chancellor' of the outlawed, Albanian-language university, **Ejup Statovci**. A camera belonging to **Natasha Bogovic**, journalist with *Danas* newspaper, was destroyed by an undercover policeman. (B92, RFE/RL)

SIERRA LEONE

A crowd brandishing machetes and sticks attacked the independent Voice of the Handicapped FM radio station in Freetown on 31 August after it broadcast a statement objecting to any form of military intervention. (Agence France Presse)

The government reiterated on 22 September that newspapers risk being shut down unless they comply with the recently-amended press law (*Index* 3/1997) which orders them to register annually. Registration costs around US$75 for new publications, US$37.50 for others, but is subject to approval by the minister of information. **Foday Fofana**, editor of *Concord* newspaper, and **Fallah Ensa-Ndemah**, acting secretary of the Sierra Leonian Association of Journalists (SLAJ), went into hiding in early October after a tip-off that they were to be arrested on subversion charges. The charges were believed to stem from SLAJ's vehement denunciation of the

military junta on 6 October and, in particular, its demand for the reregistration of newspapers. (CPJ, RSF)

Donald Davis, a freelance journalist, was arrested on charges of subversion on 8 October and detained in Pademba Road prison, Freetown. (CPJ)

David Tambaryoh, editor of *Punch* newspaper, has gone underground after being detained on 10 October for three days on charges of subversion and the 'aggravated assault' of **Ibrahim Seaga Shaw**, editor of the *Expo Times*. The subversion charge arises from Tambaryoh's alleged communication with ousted President Kabbah, UN ambassador James Jonah and John Ernest Leigh, ambassador in Washington. The assault charges, filed by Shaw, stemmed from a heated verbal disagreement during the SLAJ meeting on 6 October. (CPJ)

Freelance journalist **Abdul Salam Timbo** was arrested on charges of subversion by secret police on 10 October. He is being held incommunicado. (CPJ)

On 11 October, **John Foray**, acting editor of the *Democrat* newspaper, and freelance journalist **Abdul Kpowsa** were beaten by army officers and detained without charge in Freetown. (CPJ)

Umaru Fofana, a freelance journalist for the *Vision* newspaper and the BBC, was shot in the leg and tortured by army officers on 11

October. They claimed he was reporting for former President Tejan Kabbah's clandestine radio station, FM 98.1. He was released later that day. (CPJ)

SINGAPORE

The libel charges brought against political opponent **Benjamin Jerayetnam** by Prime Minister Goh Chok Tong were upheld in a court decision at the beginning of October. At £12,000 (US$7,360), the damages were set much lower than originally called for but the prime minister intends to press for a re-assessment. The defence QC **George Carman** accused the ruling People's Action Party of using the courts to crush political opposition. (Reuters)

SLOVAKIA

Coalition deputies on 2 September again boycotted a parliamentary session set to debate the case of deputy **Frantisek Gaulieder**, who was stripped of his mandate in December 1996 after leaving Prime Minister Vladimir Meciar's Movement for Democratic Slovakia. The special session was postponed indefinitely, despite the Constitutional Court's ruling that his expulsion was unlawful. (RFE/RL)

Bratislava municipal authorities on 2 October ordered the removal of the **Kovac Clock**, a rooftop, digital display facing the presidential palace, which counts the number of days remaining in President Kovac's five-year presidency.

(RFE/RL)

Rasto Pisko, political satirist and outspoken critic of the ruling coalition, claimed on 6 October to have been injured by an unknown assailant on 21 September. One week after the assault he was followed and received threatening phone calls. (RFE/RL)

On 8 October the cabinet adopted a bill to establish a 'helpers service' for the police force. The bill allows designated civilians to wear arm bands, carry special identity cards and empowers them to check identity documents and confiscate weapons. They will be armed with tear gas, truncheons and, in certain cases, would carry handcuffs. Former interior minister Ladislav Pittner commented that the 'price of public security should not be the emergence of a police state.' (RFE/RL)

Radio Twist, the only private station in the country, was shut down, according to a report on 13 October. Radiocommunication, a division of the state-owned Slovak Communication which owns all television and radio transmitters, said it closed the station because it had failed to pay a US$5,300 bill for use of the transmitters. A Radio Twist spokesman said the station was up-to-date in its payments and the action was politically motivated. (RFE/RL)

SOMALIA

Hassan Siad, editor of the

daily newspaper *Jamhuria*, was detained without official explanation on 8 September. The paper was shut down, with police cordoning off its printing press the following day. Siad and *Jamhuria*'s owner, **Mahmud Abdu Shide**, were accused of printing fake municipality tax receipts. They were released on 16 September and the closure order lifted. (RSF)

SOUTH AFRICA

On 4 September the Broadcasting Complaints Commission of South Africa (BCCSA) upheld a complaint against the national broadcasting corporation SABC about a Christian programme which condemned homosexuality as a sin. BCCSA found the debate was biased and one-sided. (Freedom of Expression Institute)

The telecommunications regulatory body SATRA ruled on 14 October that the parastatal Telkom did not have exclusive rights to provide internet services because it contravened the constitutional right of all South Africans to access to information. Telkom is considering challenging the ruling. (Freedom of Expression Institute)

SOUTH KOREA

Two men were arrested on 1 October for organising a human rights film festival at Hong Ik University in Seoul. The festival's sponsor **Sung-ook Yim** and a student were detained after a Seoul court issued a search warrant to ensure that the organisers had not breached legislation which requires that all films are pre-screened. The festival's organiser **Sarabang** had warned that they would not submit to pre-screening since the courts had determined in October 1996 that systematic film censorship was unconstitutional. On 19 September a Gay and Lesbian film festival, scheduled at Seoul's Yonsei University, was closed down by police and the organisers were threatened with arrest and a fine. (AI)

SRI LANKA

Journalist **DBS Jeyeraj**, now living in Canada, has received death threats from the separatist Liberation Tigers of Tamil Eelam in reaction to a column for the *Sunday Island*, in which he criticised the movement's 'stranglehold' on the Tamil community. Jeyaraj left for Canada in the mid-1980s after being detained for his writings. In 1993, he was beaten up with a baseball bat by a group of Tamil youths in Toronto, where he once edited the weekly newsletters, *Senthamarai* and *Muncharies*. On 20 August the Canada-based Tamil weekly *Muzhakkam* (Thunder) published a cartoon, which allegedly referred to the 1993 beating and urged: 'If a dog loses only a leg, it will continue to bark ... whatever job is undertaken must be completed with perfection.' Jeyaraj received threatening calls fom cellular or unlisted numbers between 29 August and 13 September. (Free Media Movement)

On 11 September parliament voted unanimously to scrap a 19-year-old law that made journalists answerable to it in cases where deputies were alleged to have been discredited by the media. The Parliamentary Privileges Special Provision Act of 1978 allowed parliament to fine and imprison journalists whose words or actions were deemed to have damaged the credibility and reputation of legislators. The act was used to fine the editors of the state-owned *Ceylon Observer* in 1978 and the Sinhala-language weekly *Ravaya* in 1991. (Reuters)

Almost eight years after the murder of journalist, human rights activist and television star **Richard de Zoysa** (*Index* 5/1990, 6/1990, 8/1990, 10/1990) on 18 February 1990, the Criminal Investigation Department took a chief inspector attached to the Anuradhapura police division and a police constable into custody on 6 October. (Peoples Liberation Front, *Daily News*)

On 6 October the Foundation for Freedom of Expression in a Democracy condemned a threat by a section of the Buddhist clergy to impose 'doctrinal sanctions' on **Mangala Samaraweera**, Minister of Posts, Telecommunications and Media, whose government seeks to end the civil war by devolving power to Tamil regions. 'It would be a sad day indeed,' said the foundation's convenor Lucien Rajakarunanayake, 'if

Buddhism is drawn into the practices of authoritarian religious leaders that seek to impose their views on the public mind, or those within their fold. (*Daily News*)

Niresh Eliatamby, correspondent for the Associated Press, was arrested by navy personnel and held for two hours following the 15 October bomb attack, allegedly by the Liberation Tigers of Tamil Eelam (LTTE), on Colombo's Galadari Hotel. Eliatamby, a Tamil, was taken to naval headquarters where a senior official checked his credentials before authorising his release. (Reuters, Voice of America)

SWAZILAND

Prime Minister Sibusiso Dlamini ordered Swaziland Television to hand over video footage of a news item on plans by trade unions to hold a meeting on 23 August, according to an anonymous source at the station. The government says the footage contains an 'illegal message'. (MISA)

A bill to regulate the media was introduced by the government on 3 October. It provides for a council, appointed by a government minister, which will license journalists and enforce a government-imposed code of ethics. On 14 and 15 October, the Swaziland Federation of Trade Unions organised a work boycott to protest the threat to the free press. Journalists are preparing a legal challenge. (MISA)

SWEDEN

The government could face thousands of legal claims for compensation because of a secret programme of forced sterilisation which was revealed at the end of August by journalist Maciej Zaremba. More than 60,000 women, some with learning difficulties, others not of pure Nordic stock, were sterilised between 1935 and 1976. There are no references to the programme in school and history books. (*Guardian, Independent*)

SYRIA

Somar al-Assad, nephew of the Syrian president and son of Vice-President Rifa'at al-Assad, launched a new Arab satellite television station in early October. Somar claimed the London-based Arab News Network had not been set up to further the ambitions of his father. Rifa'at al-Assad is best known for commanding the 1982 assault on Islamists in Homs and Hama, in which 20,000 were reported killed, and for an abortive coup attempt in the mid-1980s. A press officer working for Rifa'at, **Zubayda Muqabel**, has been detained by the security services since 7 July (*Index* 5/1997). (*Guardian*)

TAJIKISTAN

A bomb went off on the second floor of the building that houses the Tajik state news agency **Khovao** on 25 September. Several people received minor injuries in the the attack but there was extensive damage to the first

two floors of the building. The blast was attributed to an unknown group opposed to the current peace process. (RFE/RL)

Iran's official news agency IRNA accused Tajikistan on 15 October of suppressing Persian culture by closing the **Al-Mahdi** bookshop, the only one in Dushanbe that sold Persian books, and of banning signs in the Persian script. Iran and Tajikistan are linked by Persian; but while Iranians use an alphabet derived from Arabic, Tajiks write in Cyrillic. (Reuters)

TANZANIA

A recent attempt to increase HIV/AIDS awareness was cut short after the Tanzania Postal Corporation succumbed to pressure from religious groups to withdraw from circulation a stamp promoting the use of condoms. The stamp shows a sunset silhouette of a couple holding hands, with the words 'condom protects against AIDS' in Swahili and English. (*New African*)

THAILAND

A headline in the *Thai Post*, which blamed official security for the crash of a helicopter in which 14 of the Queen of Thailand's entourage were killed, could result in the newspaper being prosecuted for defamation or treason. The newspaper blamed the crash on a combination of lightning and overload. There has been no official announcement of the cause. (Institute for the Studies on Free Flow of Information)

A new constitution, which seeks to promote open and clean government, was overwhelmingly endorsed by the Thai parliament on 28 September. The package includes the country's first bill of rights and establishes special courts to hear complaints about abuse of power by politicians and officials. (*Financial Times*)

TURKEY

On 22 August, Islamists demonstrating against teaching reforms in the Laleli district of Istanbul tossed rocks and coins at journalists, shouting slogans such as 'dishonourable press'. Those who were injured or lost equipment included **Ergun Colakoglu** of *Hurriyet* and **Ahmet Sik** of the daily *Yeni Yuzyil*. In the district of Sultabeyi, journalist **Arzu Kivane** and cameraman **Onal Sondemir** with local TV station Anadolu MNG had to be taken to hospital in Taksim. (RSF)

At the eighth hearing in the **Metin Goktepe** murder trial (*Index* 2/1996, 1/1997) on 15 September, four of the officers accused of beating the *Evrensel* journalist to death in January 1996 were released by the Afyan Court of Assizes pending a verdict in the case. At the ninth hearing on 9 October, three witnesses for the prosecution attended the hearing. The court ordered the re-enactment of the crime involving all the protagonists. The next hearing was set for 9 November. (RSF, *Financial Times*)

● ●

JOHNNY WALKER

Frinton Flashing

THE studio was out on deck, so you could see out and when it was a lovely night and the moon was shining, you could see the lights on the shore. I got the engineer to fix up a long cable for the mike and the headphones. He'd stay in the studio, put the wires through the porthole and I'd go out. You could hear the chains rattling on the tyres and the water lapping against the ship. It was very atmospheric.

I started doing a communication with the listeners on shore in cars. I'd manage to isolate a car's lights and start questions and answers. This was Frinton. 'Frinton Flashing', we called it. It was really just picking out a car. I'd see one flashing and I'd say: 'I can see you flashing. Turn your lights off and now, switch them on.' And I'd pinpoint the car. And I'd say: 'Give two flashes for yes and one for no.' And then I'd ask them questions.

Were they on their own? One flash: 'No'. Are you with your girlfriend? Two flashes. Then I'd say: 'Pick the number in the alphabet of the initial letter of your name.' So I'd find out their names, how long they'd been going out together. And lots of cars would come down and also want to have a go. One night we had a BBC TV crew come out and we talked about it on the radio. 'There's this crew coming out and we want as many people as we can along the coastline.'

And I'll never forget the feeling of power, standing out on deck and saying: 'Right. Lights on!' As far as you could see for about 12 miles, the coastline was lit up by all these lights. And I'd go: 'Lights off!' And they would all go out again. It was so fantastic, such a great game.

The coast guards got very angry about that. ❑

Johnny Walker was one of the original DJs on the UK's first independent radio station, the 'pirate' Radio Caroline, which celebrated its 30th anniversary in August. He was reminiscing with **Georg Roloff.**

● ●

On 2 October, **Zeynel Bagir**, **Ismet Bakrac** and **Abdulvahap Tas** of the Diyarbakir office of the *Ulkede Gundem* were arrested while driving to the airport to pick up copies of the newspaper sent from Istanbul. The police insisted that they cease working for the daily before releasing them in the evening. In a separate incident, **Filiz Bucak** of the same newspaper's Urfa office was arrested and released on the same day. (RSF)

On 2 October, the Ankara State Security Court rejected a plea from the lawyers of imprisoned Kurdish writer **Recep Marasli** (*Index* 1/1994, 2/1994, 4/1994, 5/1994, 6/1995) that he be freed to receive medical attention. Marasli sustained permanent neurological damage when he went on hunger strike while serving his 36 year sentence on charges that he was member of the PK Rizari, a small pro-Kurdish group which produced materials promoting Kurdish political and cultural rights. Released in 1991 under a general amnesty, he was re-arrested in 1994 for speaking publicly on the Kurdish question. (PEN)

UKRAINE

Ethnic Russians in the eastern city of Donetsk staged protests against the opening of the first Ukrainian language school in the city on 1 September. Activists stated it was in response to 'forceful Ukrainisation' of the mainly Russian-speaking region. (RFE/RL)

UNITED KINGDOM

On 26 August former journalist and MI5 member of staff **David Shayler** alleged that the MI5 had kept thousands of secret files on individuals ranging from the Labour Party chief media advisor, **Peter Mandelson**, Home Office Minister **Jack Straw** and rock musician **John Lennon**. Their operations included phone tapping, mail interception and house break-ins, as recently as the early 1990s. Mr Justice Keene placed an injunction on the *Mail on Sunday* preventing it from publishing any further allegations. On 4 September at a private hearing of the High Court, the injunction was extended to prevent Shayler from making any further disclosures. (*Independent*, *Guardian*, Reuters)

The satirical fortnightly *Private Eye* attacked what it saw to be public hypocrisy over the death of Princess Diana on 31 August by running a front cover, showing a crowd trying to get hold of a newspaper containing pictures of her wrecked car. The comment led to the magazine's removal from the shelves of three retail chains and thousands of angry letters. (*Guardian*, *Independent*, *Private Eye*)

At the Eisteddford Arts Festival in Bala, Wales, where English is traditionally banned, anti-devolution campaigners were prevented from setting up their stall, verbally abused and spat upon on 15 September. (Reuters)

A portrait of convicted child murderer **Myra Hindley** was twice defaced by members of the public on 17 September, the opening day of the 'Sensation' art exhibition at London's Royal Academy. A police mug-shot of Hindley from the 1960s, now embedded in the national consciousness, had been reconstructed as a four-metre portrait by artist **Marcus Harvey**, using a stencil of a child's hand to repeat its half-tone images. The parents of Hindley's victims were outraged by the work, as was Hindley herself, who is serving a life sentence. (Reuters, *Independent*, *The Times*, *Guardian*)

It was announced on 14 September that legal protection is to be introduced for individuals who disclose crime, fraud or serious malpractice at their place of work. At the end of September, **Mike Arnold**, a communications expert at the defence ministry's Defence Evaluation Research Agency was sacked for making allegations about waste and corruption in government-managed projects. An appeal board subsequently found the dismissal 'unfair'. (*Financial Times*, *Guardian*)

Psychiatrists were told on 1 October to avoid using memory recovery techniques, such as hypnosis or regression therapy, to help victims of child sexual abuse because of the dangers of creating 'false memories'. The guidelines were issued by the Royal College of Psychiatrists which says drug-induced interviews, hypnosis and regression therapy should play no role in the unearthing of past experiences of which the patient has no awareness. (*Guardian*)

Sir Ronald Waterhouse QC ruled in mid-October that the names of the members of a paedophile ring, already implicated in systematic abuse of children at a state-run home in Wrexham, Wales, are to be kept from the public. He granted anonymity to one man, allegedly a peer, who died in 1981 and another who had twice been convicted of sexually abusing boys over a 20-year period at the same home because, he argued, it would encourage other paedophiles to collaborate with the enquiry. (*Guardian, Independent*)

USA

The Equal Employment Opportunities Commission published a National Speech Code in August, which renders remarks based on race, gender and religion in the work place 'illegal' by creating a 'hostile work environment'. **Eugene Volokh**, a free-speech teacher at University of California, condemned the government for presuming that the workplace is a 'First Amendment-free zone'. (*Washington Post*)

America On-line revealed on 15 September that it is banning artwork and essays by convicted serial killers from its system. Those denied access include Keith Hunter

Jesperson, convicted of three murders in the pacific Northwest, and Danny Rolling convicted of murdering five students in Gainesville. (*International Herald Tribune*)

On 18 September, Congress passed amendments, lobbied by the FBI and National Security Agency, to a draft of the Security And Freedom Through Encryption law (SAFE). Under the revised SAFE, any encrypted message that cannot be read by US intelligence after 2000 could earn the sender up to five years in prison. Inventors of encryption codes have frequently been chased through the courts (*Index* 2/1995, 2/1996, 4/1996). In August Judge Marilyn Hall Patel ruled in favour of **Professor Daniel Bernstein** that government licensing requirements on encryption software violated his constitutional rights to free speech. The government is expected to appeal. US firms had been unable to make or sell encryption software unless the government had 'immediate access' to the code. Codes that could not be cracked could not be exported, since they were classified under the same regulations as exports of military equipment. In August, Washington relaxed restrictions and secure codes are now advertised to non-US buyers. What is not advertised is that the code's licensee must supply a key to Washington. On 24 September a House of Representatives commerce committee approved the free

export of encryption software, rejecting the need for law enforcement agencies to be given keys to decipher messages. Without encryption a message sent via e-mail is less secure than a telephone call. It is argued that the so-called Oxley-Manton amendment to SAFE will undermine the security of cellular, digital and cordless phones. All use encryption techniques, but could be prevented from so doing after 31 January 2000. (*Guardian*)

The Central Intelligence Agency (CIA) gave up a 30-year battle in late October and disclosed how much the US spends annually on intelligence - US$26 billion. The agency was compelled to comply with the Constitution which demands that the government publish 'a regular statement and account' of its spending. The CIA spends about US$3 billion, but supplementary funds drawn down by affiliated agencies, amount to a further US$23 billion. (*International Herald Tribune*)

A member of the local Florida arts board, **Peggy McKinley**, was sacked in late September for suggesting that Cuban musicians should be allowed to play in a showcase of Latin and Caribbean music festival despite a Dade County ban. Singer **Gloria Estefan**, whose father was an officer in ousted Cuban dictator Fulgenicio Batista's regime, joined many voices against the ban. (*Independent*)

VENEZUELA

On 7 October, university student **Feliz Faria Arias** was abducted near the National University in Caracas, dragged into a car and tortured. Faria Arias is a witness to the 1991 murder of fellow student **Belinda Alvarez**. His abduction is the second attack this year, allegedly by members of the Direccion de los Servicios de Intelligencia y Prevencion. (AI)

VIETNAM

Imprisoned writer **Pham Duc Kham** was released on 28 August, five years before his sentence was due to expire. He was imprisoned in 1990 on charges of 'attempting to overthrow the people's power' through his involvement in publishing an unauthorised newspaper, *Freedom Forum*. The interior ministry said that Kham was being freed for 'humanitarian reasons'. On 16 September, the foreign ministry issued a statement saying that there are no prisoners detained for the expression of their views. (PEN)

Journalists were barred from providing foreign reporters with information without the approval of the authorities in a decree passed on 6 October. Foreign news bureaux were also banned from hiring local journalists. (RSF)

Newspaper editor **Nguyen Hoang Linh** was arrested in early October for divulging state secrets and could face between seven to 15 years in jail under the criminal code. Linh published a series of articles in May alleging that customs officials had been involved in corruption during purchases of patrol boats. (Reuters)

YEMEN

On 17 September, **Ahmad Abdalla Al Sufi**, secretary general of the Yemen Institute of Democratic Development, was searched and 'humiliated' while departing for a flight to Cairo. The authorities are said to have confiscated paper, documents and files relating to the institute and a book he had written, ostensibly on the unfair conduct of elections. (OMCT)

ZAMBIA

On 2 September the Lusaka community radio station Radio Phoenix was banned from relaying live BBC programmes on the grounds that it was in breach of licence. The station was gutted by fire on 18 September but resumed broadcasting in early October. (MISA)

Dickson Jere, **Reuben Phiri**, **George Chilembo** and **Amos Malupenga**, journalists with the daily *Post*, were ordered at gunpoint to leave Lusaka airport on 8 September. Army officers confiscated their camera equipment. Journalists from state-owned media, who were covering the departure to London of Chief Litunga of Barotseland, were not troubled. (MISA)

The *Post* received a telephone call on 19 September in which an anonymous voice threatened to burn down its offices. The caller advised the paper to draw lessons from the fate of Radio Phoenix. (MISA)

ZIMBABWE

Three Zambian journalists, **Kalinda Shachinda** of the state-owned *Daily Mail*, **Mudenda Hacilima** of the Zambia Information Service (ZIS) and **Ruth Banda** of the independent *Post*, were thrown out of a meeting between Zambian and Zimbabwean tourism officials for asking 'nagging' questions. (MISA)

★★★

Compiled by: Penny Dale (Africa); Andrew Kendle, Nicky Winstanley-Torode (Asia); Simon Martin, Vera Rich (eastern Europe & CIS); Neil Durkin (south America); Nevine Mabro (central America); Rupert Clayton, M Siraj Sait (Middle East); Randip Panesar (north America and Pacific); Jessie Banfield (UK & western Europe)

Partitions: divide and quit

As a solution to conflict, it seldom brings lasting peace, leaves injustice in its wake and never resolves the sources of hostility. In India it was achieved at an intolerable human cost. Yet today partition has been dusted off once more to become the 'least bad' solution to the failures of contemporary politics. From Ireland to Bosnia, *Index* asks: Why partition?

Israel/Egypt border: families communicate through the barbed wire of partition
Credit: JC Tordai/Panos

ZLATKO DIZDAREVIC

Sarajevo

I KNOW nothing of the dramatic 50-year-old story of the exodus of Pakistanis from India except what I can read in newspapers and books; nor of the human suffering in Cyprus, Korea, Vietnam. I know a little more about Palestine and Israel because I know people there. You carry the books on departures, partitions, lost homes along with the remembrance of your own home within yourself until the end of your days. As told and heard by others, the story of your lost home usually has little to do with what you would really want to say.

However, I believe I do know something about Bosnia and our homes, our past and our future. And it has nothing to do with politics, history or the world outside.

I understand the story of 9 January 1994, when, in the midst of the war, my father died. It was one of these days when people 'from the hill' tried to chase us out of town, simply because we had the 'wrong names', or 'didn't fit' with their madness; or because we couldn't be incorporated into new maps drawn somewhere else.

On that dreadful, cold morning of January 1994, I wrote, for myself, on a scrap of paper, a short story about father's funeral. Maybe it has no connection with those Pakistanis, Cypriots, Kurds, Koreans or Palestinians: that cannot and will not happen here. Or maybe there is a connection.

My story goes like this.

AFTER ALL THIS I have only one wish: that my sons Ognjen and Drazen, Sarajevans and Europeans by luck or sheer circumstance, turn out like their grandfather. My father. A man killed by 'natural' causes on 9 January 1994, after he himself decided it should be that way. I don't know if my sons will achieve this; its so difficult. But even if they try, it will mean a lot to us, though mainly to them.

The night before he was laid to rest in the Lion Cemetery, where all honourable Sarajevans are buried, my father lay dead in his apartment, a place he didn't want to leave even when he could. Under a huge, somewhat naive painting of the Old Bridge at Mostar, over the unrealistically blue river Neretva. All his life he carried that painting within him. Finally, he painted it. As a painter he was an amateur but his love for that city and river was most professional, so he painted seriously and with great care. That night his bed was surrounded by neighbours who were unknown to the family. They came when they heard of his death, only asking if they could sit around him. 'That's the least we can do for a man like him. We don't know how to tell you how much he meant to us, how nicely he spoke with us...' I remembered that my father had asked me for cigarettes during the past months, even though he didn't smoke. 'For my friends from the block,' he would say. 'You know, Zlatko, they don't have any.' It was then that I saw his friends from the block for the first time, at his bed on his last day in the house, under the painting of the Old Bridge. It was an honour to have the kind of friends Mustafa Dizdarevic had: a high-ranking officer of an army that was finished a long time ago, a carpenter, a trolley conductor, a retired cook.

The day before he went to bed for the last time, my father told me why he had decided not to get up again. I didn't understand any of the most important things about this war. He saw me to the door and hugged me. We never hugged after visits to my parents. We had something of a 'macho' relationship: as a child he taught me that men didn't display their feelings but that it was their duty to carry their love for people within themselves, without showing it too openly. This, of course, loosened up with old age, when he stole kisses from my sons, his grandchildren.

That day I saw all the pictures of his grandchildren I had brought for him during the war from their places of exile. They were neatly lined up in the china cupboard in his room. I didn't understand the message he tried to get across with those pictures. But there was a message. At the doorstep, he told me: 'Zlatko, its over. My time has come. I will never again see Ognjen and Drazen, they've destroyed my Old Bridge near the place I grew up, and I can't even hear my violin any more.' He had that violin for 73 years. The violin itself was more than 120-years-old. Five years ago, during happier times, he had bequeathed it to his grandson Drazen. He claimed that 'the boy most certainly had a good ear for music...'

I thought it was a passing thing. He was strong and could still stand on his feet. I didn't realise at the time that no one can stand on their feet if they have had their grandchildren, the very meaning of days to come, taken away from them by force; if the memory of their childhood, as the very meaning of their past, has been taken away from them; and if their violin, as the very sense of the present, has also been taken away. My mother 'phoned the next morning and couldn't say anything. She cried, and only then did I begin to understand why he had broken his rule the day before by hugging me.

Death by 'natural' causes in Sarajevo has a hidden and cruel meaning. My father was not killed by a bullet or a piece of shrapnel intended to damage his body. 'They' spared his heart and his head, but they took away something even more precious: they robbed him of his past, future and present. A day later they 'dug him in' at the Lion Cemetery, at '1.45pm'. That's what was written on a coffin made out of some kind of thick cardboard.

Sarajevo: 'They did not kill him with a bullet...they spared his heart and his head; but they took away his past, his present and his future'Credit Kevin Weaver

The price – 75 marks and five litres of gas. I screamed like crazy at 1.15pm, telling them not to start the burial because they had said it was '1.45pm', and it was too early. I was still waiting for some other friends of his to come, bakers and generals, fishermen, musicians and journalists. Then the gravediggers shouted from further down, 'Either you get down here or we'll start filling in. What we do care about time. They kill around here, man'.

That's how he was 'dug in'. A vault bought long ago and now overgrown with weeds, not far from the gaping absence of the Old Bridge, will remain empty forever. The bakers, the generals, the fishermen and the musicians came at exactly 1.45pm, as they had been told. It was too late – for the funeral, for tears, for silence.

Everybody who says you die in Sarajevo the way you lived is a big liar. In Sarajevo, in fact, life ends only by killing. By 'natural' killing and regular killing. After the killing, however, grandchildren stay on to resemble the killed. Grandchildren who are Sarajevans and, only through sheer circumstance, Europeans. And for these grandchildren, a violin.

After five years in Italy where he grew up, Ognjen is back in Sarajevo. One day he simply told me: 'I want to know where my home is, I want to have friends here. I want to be Sarajevan.' He also wanted to go to Mostar to visit the non-existent Old Bridge, painted by his grandfather. He asked me, 'Where am I going to be buried?' It was a naive child's question uttered in a most natural way by someone for whom death had no reality. Surprised, I answered, 'Well, here in Sarajevo. This is our home.' 'That's the way it should be,' was his only comment.

Younger son Drazen is still in Italy. Some time ago he asked for the violin which his grandfather had left him. 'I want to have it with me, I want to show it to everybody here, in Italy, the violin of my grandfather from Sarajevo.'

Last year, Drazen, now 11-years-old, didn't mention returning to Sarajevo. Recently, he sent a letter to his older brother, Ognjen. 'Take good care of our home. More and more often I think of getting there, same as you did.'

Does partition ever work? Except what can be read in newspapers and books, I know nothing of that. ❑

Zlatko Dizdarevic is the editor of Svijet *magazine*

RADHA KUMAR

A bridge too far

Partition never did solve anything – unless at great price. Yet today, 50 years after the old 'divide and quit' formula was first applied to British India, it is being dusted off and reapplied to the newest 'ethnic' problems

DOWN by the edge of the walled town in Nicosia, there is a clear stretch of wire mesh separating the free from the occupied territories. This is the only clearly demarcated stretch of border: in the rest of the old town the green line dividing the city is marked by sandbags and oil cans, seeming at first sight an *ad hoc* and casual partition. Indeed at one point it is marked by a locked blue wooden door beyond which lies a vacant lot bordering a street strewn with debris. Like a child in a Victorian fairy tale, I rattle the door and peer through the gap between door and post. It would be so easy to climb over and walk through that portentous street kicking debris, chancing on an old photograph or a torn book. But along the street a soldier watches from behind an oil can and on the other side of the street Turkish and Turkish-Cypriot flags fly from a minaret. The buffer zone is so narrow here, says Nikos, a rebel physicist who has taken me under his wing for the afternoon, that UN patrol helicopters, whose air space must exactly match the borders of the buffer zone, frequently risk fire by blundering over one or other line.

Barbed wire is the most commonly chosen image of partitioned societies, and on the World Wide Web the home page of the free Cyprus Republic opens with just such an image. But the home page of the occupied Turkish Republic of North Cyprus opens with a map of the divided island in which happy faces spill out of the northern section while the south is an empty white block. This surprising juxtaposition is suddenly not so surprising down by our stretch of clear mesh. Here the Turkish side is atop a grassy wall overlooking the road on the Greek-

The bridge at Mostar – Credit: A. Boulat/Rex

Cypriot side. There are groups of Turkish-Cypriots and Anatolian peas-
ants strolling on the grass, pressing their faces to the mesh, calling a
greeting. But on the Greek-Cypriot road, down below, we are the only
pedestrians.

The Greek-Cypriots gather at a different stretch of the green line, by
the entrance to the UN headquarters in the buffer zone. This no-man's
land is populated by UN agencies and personnel, and it is a green
enclave of tennis and football courts, wide rolling roads and water
sprinklers. The entrance, however, is a sandbagged alley, and here Greek-
Cypriot refugee organisations have mounted a permanent exhibit
mourning people killed in encounters with Turkish-Cypriot forces.
Every weekend Greek-Cypriots demonstrate at the two checkpoints to
deter tourists from crossing over into the north; to pass through the
Turk-Cypriot checkpoints on the other side, they say, is tantamount to

recognising Raul Denktash's rogue state.

Partition lines have an unhappy knack of gathering scattered animosities into one virulent strain. The *auto de fe* with which Serbs fled the Sarajevo suburbs following the Dayton Peace Agreement of 1995 was searing because it spoke of their deep belief that they were loathed and their desperate readiness to be loathsome. The destruction of the bridge over the Neretva in Mostar, for centuries one of the great artifacts of Ottoman syncretism, was such a potent symbol of the way in which the Bosnian war ravaged Europe itself that the European Union's first major undertaking following the 1994 Washington agreement was to rebuild it. The gesture was an empty one. For close on three years an EU administration laboured to reopen bridges between east and west Mostar – and cost the international community several million dollars – yet the one attempt to arrange a visit by Muslims from east Mostar to a cemetery in west Mostar was met by an armed attack by a Hercegovinian rabble (including local government and police officials). Indeed, it was under the EU administration that Hercegovinian ethnic nationalists continued the effort to push the Mostar partition line from the west bank of the river.

Throughout its tenure, the EU administration was little better than a moneylender without the power to extract interest or enforce payment. It accepted the mandate of reunifying Mostar but its chosen interlocutors were the ethnic nationalist mafias who had run the Croat-Muslim war. This, they said, was because the EU had to work with elected parties; otherwise, it might be accused of behaving like a colonial power. As a result, they had no authority to prevent the continuing expulsion of Muslims; and their own feeble police force was frequently held up by Croat gangs.

Yet the Neretva river is not a no-man's land and is unlikely ever to become one. The Bosnian war did not create one but hundreds of little disconnected partition lines, which begin and end abruptly at city limits, bridges or erstwhile road and rail junctions. Ironically, it is the Dayton Agreement that has provided a continuous partition line (though it is broken at Brcko), and it is the NATO-led Stabilisation Forces (SFOR) that might create a no-man's land in Bosnia. The tragedy of partitions is that no-man's lands are established in a sort of peace – little more than a separation of forces – not in war. And because they are buffer zones rather than a border, they keep a simmering hostility alive indefinitely.

Borders, after all, can be crossed; no-man's lands cannot.

The US and NATO role in Bosnia points up a curious truth about ethnic partitions: no matter how deep or violent hostilities might be the agreement to partition is always made at third-party intervention. Classically a colonial formula, ethnic partition was a particular favourite of the British, who pushed it through in Ireland, threatened it in Cyprus, proposed it in Palestine and claimed it as a crowning achievement of the Raj in India. Writing in 1937 to propose the partition of Palestine, it was an Oxbridge don, Reginald Coupland, who produced the inimitable rationale: 'Where the conflict of nationalities has been overcome and unity achieved – in Britain itself, in Canada, in South Africa – one of the parties concerned was English or British, and...where that has not been so, as in the schism between the Northern and Southern Irish, or between Hindus and Muslims in India, the quarrel, though it is centuries old, has not yet been composed.' (Palestine Royal Commission Report, 1937). European Jews, he added, could not be expected to live with Arabs.

In the event, it was not the British but the Zionists who partitioned Palestine, but in such a way that one new state, Israel, was created without a corresponding Palestinian one. Sadly, Israel proved Coupland right. In 1967, it simply occupied the West Bank outright, treating its inhabitants as at best sub-human and at worst invisible. To this extent, the entire West Bank could be seen as a vast no-man's land. Arguably, the 1992-93 Oslo Accords' single great achievement was to force recognition that this no-man's land was in fact full of men, women and children. But having done so, Oslo also introduced a form of divide and rule politics into the West Bank, first by offering the Palestinian authority a notional mandate while Israel continued to control all essential aspects of rule, including roads and water, and then by pouring resources into the ghettoised set of institutions the authority comprised, so that they became bloated and self-serving.

Predictably, it is in the security arena that the Oslo divide and rule is most revealing. Here Israel plays cox and box with Hamas and the Palestinian Authority: while the latter are supposed to police the former, Israel itself can simultaneously attempt to assassinate one Hamas leader and release another. In effect, this means that the Palestinian Authority's role is to target the frustrated youth who provide Hamas support, while Israel deals with the leadership. Yet the way Oslo is playing out has also instituted a form of divide and rule within Israel, with Russian Jews being pitted against European and US Jews as settlers versus modernists, or fundamentalists versus reformists. The question now is whether there is a third party with sufficient will to force a completion of Palestine's incomplete partition, but since the only involved party with any colonial semblance is Israel itself, the chances seem slim.

Unlike Bosnians or Cypriots, the Palestinians have now arrived at a point where they are prepared to accept partition as the price of independence. Surprisingly, India-Pakistan is the only other case in which independence was bought at the same price. While the wounds of up to 2 million dead and 16 million displaced are not easily healed, India, Pakistan and Bangladesh have been able to take a minimal but crucial step which most other partitioned states have not. No-man's land has gradually become a border rather than a buffer zone. How much this can mean is evidenced by the widespread soul-searching this fiftieth anniversary – and in particular, by the choice of the Wagah canal as potent symbol of our loss and our conjoint history.

Growing up in partitioned India, I had crossed the border into Pakistan by train but I had never stood at the Wagah canal (on the Punjab border) which is our equivalent of the Nicosia stretch of clear mesh. The gathering of Indians and Pakistanis at the Wagah canal on Independence Day this year has been widely publicised in articles and speeches at home and abroad. But few have mentioned that this was the place where writers and painters gathered in an attempt to protest the partition of Punjab in 1947. Fikr Tausvi, who wrote about that attempt, spoke bitterly of the desert that the area had become a few years later; were he alive perhaps he would feel that this year's references show that something of the spirit of the attempt has, after all, influenced the way his countrymen – both Indian and Pakistani – feel about the Wagah canal. Certainly as a symbol it stands in sharp distinction to the earthed-over memories of other areas, which are gradually, or – as in my case – accidentally, being excavated by historians today.

Last year, researching Partition in the India Office Library, I chanced on a pamphlet which offered a grim aside on the link we had made between the horrors of partition and the pogrom against the Sikhs. In my city, Delhi, the worst attacks on Sikhs had taken place in the outlying areas of east Delhi. The reason why there was a concentration of Sikhs here, the pamphlet told me, was because in 1947 Sikhs fleeing partitioned Punjab had, together with extremist Hindu nationalists, massacred and driven out the Muslim settlers of these areas.

The chilling layers of self-censorship which swaddle us in south Asia are less buried but equally dismaying in Kashmir, the only place where no-man's land not only continues but is constantly recreated. At the height of the government-militant conflict, when the valley was under siege, the number of stories in the Indian press on the human-suffering of this war could be counted on the fingers of one hand. Yet these, we claimed, were our countrymen. Only the exceptional Pakistani will consider the expulsion of Hindus from the valley a misfortune. And in Kashmir itself, I have yet to hear a single supporter of independence discuss the aspirations of the Ladakhi Buddhists, who inhabit over 50 per cent of the state's territory.

Today, in the wake of the Dayton Peace Agreement, there is a rising belief that partition might be the best of bad solutions to ethnic conflict. The truth is that ethnic partition not only prolongs conflict indefinitely, it can also institutionalise it at the most intimate levels. Look at Belfast, a criss-cross of buffer zones and no-man's lands, a concentration of Ireland's partition to the point where peace will now stand or fall according to what that ravaged city upholds.

On the fiftieth anniversary of India's Partition, it is terrible to think that the failed colonial formula of ethnic partition is being dusted off to fit Bosnia, where partition is not even the price of independence. Even more terrible to think that this partition could be stabilised by NATO, the erstwhile Cold War institution, whose first major mission is Bosnia, and whose expansion is actually playing out in Bosnian fields. ❏

Radha Kumar is an Indian writer currently engaged in research in the USA

CHRISTOPHER HITCHENS

First find your fault-line

The partition of Cyprus demonstrates both the art and science of dividing even the smallest of nations

THE modern theory and practice of partition is of two distinct kinds. The first involves the post-colonial partition, whereby apparently irreconcilable differences between subject peoples are arbitrated by the colonial power on its way out. Divide and rule – which is a method of administration – becomes, in its decadent phase, a means of orderly withdrawal. The distinguished colonial civil servant Sir Penderel Moon summarised this historical irony in the title of his book *Divide and Quit*. And thus we have the partition of Ireland, which also involved the partition of Ulster from nine counties into six and three; the partition of India, which also involved the partition of Bengal and the Punjab; the partition of Palestine and so on. With the British, this became almost a tic. First they said they would never leave. Then they said that partition would be the last thing they did. Then they left, and partition *was* the last thing they did. They proposed the partition of Eritrea after 1945 and, through the agency of Lord Carrington, the partition of South Africa in the dying years of apartheid (which is, in effect, the Afrikaans word for partition).

The second variety of partition involves the Cold War, rather than any address to the resolution of internal or tribal disputes. The division of Germany, Vietnam and Korea was and is of this kind, and arose from demarcation disputes between the superpowers as well as (especially in the case of Vietnam) unresolved post-colonial issues. Again the British were to the fore, in having their own zone in Germany and a continuing interest in the division of the country; in being one of the leading lieutenants of the US-led United Nations intervention in Korea and in being, in the case of Vietnam, the authors of the partition at Geneva in 1954. It was Sir Anthony Eden who first suggested a North and South division to Dulles and Eisenhower. (One can almost picture him saying: 'Try it. It's what we always do when we can't think of anything else.') The only instance of a British territory with an internal intercommunal dispute where partition has not been the strong recommendation of London is that of Canada – presumably because in that case partition would be to the benefit of the French.

In the case of Cyprus, in the 1950s the British embarked on a partitionist strategy that was a blend of both the colonial and the Cold War styles. Here was a small but strategic island, anchored off partitioned Palestine, and adjacent to the Suez Canal zone (itself an amputation from occupied Egypt) that had provided the lifeline to now-partitioned India. The majority community – the 82 per cent or so who spoke Greek – wanted either to unify with Greece or to become independent. The minority community, some 18 per cent, spoke Turkish. (Tiny groups of Armenians and Maronites

made up the difference.) Faced with a rebellion by the majority, the British had to balance, or manipulate, majority rights versus minority rights, and the interests of Greece and Turkey as countries, as well as the interest of NATO as an alliance which included both Athens and Ankara.

There is an art and a science to partition. The art consists in representing yourself as caught between irreconcilable forces, as the hapless and neutral mediator. This plays well with uninstructed public opinion at home, and makes for facile cartoons of, say, a vessel of statesmanship caught between Scylla and Charybdis. Who will blame you if, in the end, you throw up your hands and say that the role of disinterested referee is too difficult to sustain? The science, meanwhile, consists in identifying and exacerbating such elements of intercommunal discord as can be made (without risking a complete breakdown of law and order) to suit your book. Each bloody incident that arises from part two will, deliciously enough, reinforce your position under the heading of part one. (Those who remember the alternation between 'safe havens' and folded arms in Bosnia, or the invocation of 'ancient hatreds' as opposed to international law, will have little difficulty in seeing this point.)

In order to justify this suspicion in the case of Cyprus, one would have to be able to show that the British authorities (a) encouraged the Turkish minority to think that it would benefit from taking a rejec-

'Women Walk Home', a 1989 protest march into Turkish-occupied Cyprus from the UN buffer zone – Credit: Pam Isherwood/Format

tionist line and (b) supported those within that minority who took the most extreme position. As with the Orangemen in 1913 and the Muslim League in 1946, the weight of evidence is that the British knew a 'strategic minority' when they saw one. To give just a few examples:

- The colonial authorities in Cyprus forbade the display of the Greek flag and banned all Greek political parties. But they allowed the open formation of the 'Cyprus is Turkish Party', headed and financed by a Turkish mainland agent named Hikmet Bil.
- Harold Macmillan, as UK Foreign Secretary, argued in Cabinet for 'stirring up the Turks' to neutralise majority anti-colonial agitation. The Tory MP CM Woodhouse, a relative by marriage of the Churchill family, records the fact in his memoirs and regrets his failure to prevent it.
- The first intercommunal violence in Cyprus – a bomb outside the Turkish consulate in Nicosia, leading to vicious anti-Greek rioting – was in fact a provocation by Turkish extremists. This has been admitted, on film, by their ultra-nationalist leader Rauf Denktash. At the time the bombing was used by the British as a pretext to repress the Greek majority further. Denktash was then, and remains to this day, an especial favourite of the British Foreign Office.
- The Turkish government was encouraged, at international meetings on the crisis, to demand that if the British departed, the island should revert to Turkish sovereignty. (It had been part of the Ottoman Empire until 1878.)

There was a fatal flaw, however, in the British approach. As a colonial partition model, it functioned smoothly and predictably enough. But it took insufficient notice of the Cold War dimension. The United States, newly arrived as the post-Suez regional superpower, wanted more of a balance between Greek and Turkish mainland interests, and more 'sensitivity' to the anti-colonial mood at the United Nations. Under this and other pressures, the British hastily negotiated a partitionist Cyprus constitution, which built in and entrenched the old British and Turkish colonial distinctions between 'Muslim' and 'non-Muslim' and left the island to its probable fate while retaining 100 square miles of prime real estate as inalienable British military territory.

[A note here, which is not a digression. In 1980, during the Lancaster House negotiations on the independence of Zimbabwe, I had occasion to call on the London office of the 'Turkish Federated State of Cyprus'. Their then-representative proudly invited me into his private office. Seated within was the delegation of the Smith-Muzorewa regime to the talks, or rather the

Matabeleland contingent of it, headed by Chief Kaisa Ndeweni. They told me that, in the event of a Mugabe or Patriotic Front victory, they would try and partition 'Rhodesia' between the Shona and the Ndebele. British and South African sympathy might be available. They wanted to talk to the Turks about how it was done. The Lancaster House talks had actually opened with a speech from the Patriotic Front spokesman, warning that any attempt to foist a 'Cyprus constitution' on the country would be resisted.]

Within a very short time of taking over the dominant position on the island, the USA had decided on a partitionist solution of its own. However, this was to be a partition between Greece and Turkey, not between Greek and Turkish Cypriots. (The essential distinction was lost upon those who viewed the island as essentially uninhabited, and its people as a sort of blank map from the air, ready to have lines drawn through them.) WH Auden caught this mentality very well in his mordant 1947 poem about Lord Radcliffe's hasty plan for the dismemberment of India:

Unbiased at least he was when he arrived on his mission
Having never set eyes on this land he was called to partition
Between two peoples fanatically at odds
With their different diets and incompatible gods.

Returning to home base, the proconsul 'quickly forged the case, as a good lawyer must'. An essential element in the 'forging' of the case about Cyprus was the contention that only partition could bring peace to irreconcilable factions. In fact, those who favoured partition were exactly those who were most in favour of war, both civil and national.

Cyprus under the presidency of Archbishop Makarios pursued a course of 'non-alignment', maddening to NATO. This policy had the tacit support of the island's large and Communist-dominated labour movement. In many villages and municipalities, Greek and Turkish Cypriots continued to live close together and be members of the same trade unions and cultural associations. It was the particular task of the Greek Cypriot nationalist Right, and of its Turkish counterpart, to break up this solidarity and to create siege mentalities in both communities. And it is a matter of documented record that both EOKA-B and the TMT received their finance, their armament, their leadership and their training from outside Cyprus. Much of that encouragement came from the US Central Intelligence Agency, which subsidised both kinds of local fascist in the name of anti-Communist warfare.

The fallout was not confined to Cyprus itself. The two leading fascist politicians in both Greece and Turkey – General George Grivas and Colonel

British UN troops and Australian police guard the Cyprus buffer zone in Nicosia, 1996 – Credit: Alistair Mills

Alparslan Turkes, respectively – were both Cypriots. They demonstrated my hypothesis about nationalism being strongest at the periphery (Hitler the Austrian, Bonaparte the Corsican, Karadzic the Montenegrin etc). Both Greece and Turkey were edged towards dictatorship, in the 1960s and 1970s, by military and political forces that had been set in motion by the Cyprus conflict. Certainly, one reason for NATO's tolerance of the Greek *junta* was the promise it gave of overthrowing Makarios. And a reason for similar tolerance of subsequent Turkish military dictatorships was the fact that these had accomplished the same objective – partition – albeit in a somewhat different and more arbitrary form.

The present form of Turkish-imposed partition is inherently unstable because it directly reverses the actual proportions of population to territory, and because it increasingly threatens the actual physical annexation of northern Cyprus to Turkey. These conditions make it impossible for any Greek mainland or Greek Cypriot government to countersign a division of the island and, as a result, have spurred an arms race which eats up an irrational proportion of the social product of all three countries. Nonetheless, short-sighted western policy has up to now, because of its dogma about partition, considered any partition to be safer and more manageable than none. It is quite common to hear State Department and Foreign Office people refer casually to 'North Cyprus' and 'South Cyprus', as if the *fait accompli* had already been confirmed by international law. But in point of fact, with most of the water resources in the north and most of the citrus in the south, for example, there is no economic logic to partition. And a separation of communities can only be brought about by mass deportation and expulsion. Nor can an island so small support two state machines, unless one of them is simply the colonial extension of the mainland power. Finally, and most absurdly, Cyprus is very near the front of the queue of entrants to the European Union. Greece is already a member and Turkey is a supplicant for membership. Ankara has declared, with the endorsement of Denktash, that if the Republic of Cyprus is admitted, then it will directly integrate occupied Cyprus into Turkey proper. Thus a Cypriot passport would become valid for travel, work and residence anywhere in any European Union country except Cyprus! And the Turkish Cypriots would have to wait for the thus long-postponed accession of Turkey to the EU before they could hope to share in the benefits of membership. Meanwhile, the danger of war within Europe and within NATO would have very greatly increased.

I have been across the Berlin Wall at Checkpoint Charlie and across the Jordan at the Allenby Bridge. I have been to Panmunjom and along the line, sown with nuclear mines, that divides the Koreas. I have crossed checkpoints at the Irish border by road and rail. I have used the only land checkpoint between India and Pakistan, on the Grand Trunk Road between Lahore and Amritsar. But I've never seen anything as intrinsically ridiculous as the line which runs through the middle of Nicosia. Here is something that seems to represent the negation of everything that 'Europe' claims to stand for. Partition may seem an odd choice of subject for a magazine like *Index*. But it's not just that one cannot be indifferent to the standards and conduct of the larger geopolitics. It's that partition requires partitionism and indeed partitionists, and that these forces, which claim to take human nature at its worst and fatalistically, in fact rely on the instilling and inculcation of tribalism, on the elevation of the state and the race above humanism, and on atavistic loyalty and the suppression of critical and inquiring thought. The abolition of artificial frontiers is, so to speak, an aim well within our province. ❑

Christopher Hitchens' book Cyprus: Hostage To History *has just been reissued in paperback by Verso*

JOHN O'FARRELL

Reinventing partition

Politically, the partition of Ireland has been a dismal failure; culturally it has succeeded beyond the wildest dreams of its instigators

IRELAND has long been a Petri dish for British experiments in governance. The plantations of surplus populations from thé 'mainland' in the sixteenth and seventeenth centuries was a precursor to subsequent colonial policy in North America and the Antipodes. More recently, Northern Ireland has seen innovations in the relations between subjects and state, from proportional representation in local and European elections, to advanced surveillance and the removal of the right to silence.

The biggest innovation of all was partition. Faced with a clear demand for self-government from the island's (mainly Catholic) majority, countered by a threat of armed insurrection from its (mainly Protestant) minority, the British government of Lloyd George negotiated a Treaty in 1921 with Sinn Fein which granted separate dominion status to the two parts of a divided island. The six northern counties became Northern Ireland, while the 26 remaining counties became the Irish Free State.

This ethnopolitical partition was based on a religious headcount, with the majority of Protestants living in the North. It was also based on the economic viability of the province. Despite the use of the term 'Ulster' to describe its boundaries, the writ of the border ignored the historical nine-county size of that ancient province. It also ignored the fact that only four of the counties held clear Protestant majorities. This was a severe quandary for unionists such as Edward Carson, who believed that the union with Britain was best for all of Ireland, not just part of it. Furthermore, the 70,000 Protestants in the remaining three counties excluded from the north were 'abandoned' to the Catholic 'Rome rulers'. A nine-county Ulster would have given a Protestant majority of

British troops protecting an Orangemen march through Catholic Portadown – Credit: Gilles Peres/Magnum Photos

56 per cent, too frail to control. The 66 per cent majority in the truncated six counties felt much more secure. As a journalist and Unionist
MP of the time put it: 'If a ship were sinking and there were only
enough lifeboats for two thirds of the passengers, should they all drown
rather than leave anyone behind?'

Michael Collins, who negotiated the Treaty on behalf of the IRA
and was killed defending it shortly after, despaired: 'Who will not say
that from Britain's policy it is the North-East which has suffered most?
...She might have gained real wealth as a sturdy and independent section
of the population. She exchanged it for a false ascendancy over her
countrymen, which has brought her nothing but dishonour. A large portion of her fair province has lost all its native distinctiveness. It has
become merely an inferior Lancashire. That is the unhappy fate of the
North-East. It is neither English nor Irish.'

From that early stage, it seems clear that the iron of *realpolitik* had
entered the souls of those who publicly espoused the 'freedom to
achieve freedom' while preparing to drop all claims to the six counties.
From the initial organisation of the Free State, through its Catholic
Canon Law-inspired constitution of 1937, to the declaration of the
Republic in 1949, to the Downing Street Declaration of 1993, the
South let the North proceed apace, relatively unmolested apart from
some half-hearted incursions from what remained of the IRA, until
1969. Even when the 'Troubles' erupted, southern support for northern
Catholics was viewed as highly subversive, with successive Dublin governments employing a range of repressive measures against troublesome
republicans. From 1921 until now, no Irish government has ever made
serious contingency plans in case the rhetoric became real, and the state
expanded to five million people.

For many southerners the North became inexplicable and boring.
News reports seemed filled with violence and bile, with no possibility of
a civilised solution. As a primary schoolchild in the late 1960s, I was
taught that the North was 'the fourth green field', rightfully ours and
stolen by the Saxons. By the time I started secondary school in the
1970s, things were complicated by the emergence of a revisionist wave
of historians, many of whom were in the coalition government of the
day. Conor Cruise O'Brian, Garret Fitzgerald and John A Murphy led a
hegemonic shift in how the modern history of Ireland was perceived,
from the use of arms to the development of the Republic to its relations

with the North.

This cultural partition was reinforced by the realities of 70 years of separation. We in the South ate different sweets, smoked different cigarettes, watched different television. They in the North had things we poor southerners could only envy, such as a comprehensive free health service and welfare state, good roads and large manufacturing industries. Their Protestantism seemed exotic and strange to those of us who rarely met a 'prod', and those few we knew were nice Anglicans, not those fire-breathing Free Presbyterians we laughed at on TV. Eventually 'our' Ireland became the 26 counties. The Celtic Tiger economy, Mary Robinson, our new liberal laws – such as the right to divorce, abortion, laws protecting gay rights and, in 1997, the Freedom of Information Act – the decline of the Catholic church, even U2: our proud symbols which we boast about at every available opportunity, are firmly rooted outside the North. This is why, for most southerners, Seamus Heaney is more 'Irish' and less 'northern' than his classmate John Hume. Heaney has lived for many years in Dublin; Hume remained in Derry, neither English nor Irish.

We are not alone in our sense of separation. That northern Protestants neither know nor care about their southern neighbours comes as little surprise. But what surprised me when I moved from Dublin to Belfast almost four years ago was the hostility northern nationalists felt towards the South. They felt abandoned, left to the untender mercies of a 'Protestant parliament for a Protestant people' (to quote a Northern Ireland prime minister) which harassed and maltreated them with as much vigour as southern governments persecuted the minority there that tried to support northern Catholics. In the period around partition, Protestant paramilitaries became state-sanctioned death squads, known as the B Specials, who murdered and burnt out Catholics as a pre-emptive measure lest the IRA campaign in the south spread to the six counties. Gerrymandering was rife in the one-party state based in Stormont, along with blatant job discrimination and rigorously enforced cultural repression. The start of the 'Troubles' marked the point at which northern Catholics decided enough was enough.

But 'both sides' share much in common. There is a common mentality of siege and mistrust, and a peculiar unwillingness to acknowledge present realities. 'Both sides' still refer to the 'Irish Free State' almost 50 years after the Republic of Ireland Act. There are common misconceptions about the social character of the Republic, a belief that Rome still rules. The rapid economic changes of the 1990s, with per capita GNP overtaking the UK, are ignored in favour of an outdated image of rural poverty.

The real partition story has moved on. There is now more cross-border traffic in humanity and capital than ever before. Until late 1994, there were just six road crossings. Now, the old blown-up bridges are being repaired and the reinforced concrete pillars removed, usually by local farmers and Sinn Fein activists, supported by Catholic and Protestant businessmen who see an economic as much as a nationalist logic in reconnecting border towns with their natural hinterlands, on both sides of the fence.

While the partition of Ireland may have failed politically, culturally it has succeeded beyond the wildest dreams of its perpetrators. Northern Ireland is going through a process of repartition. 'Benign apartheid', to quote a human rights activist, is the reality of life here. Prods and Taigs, as we call each other, go to different schools, use different sets of names, have different views on the peace process, play different games, listen to different music and generally live in different areas. Mixed areas are generally shrinking. Community relations activists believe that we are less reconciled since the ceasefires of 1994, as shown by the effective Protestant uprising around the Drumcree parade in 1996, and the uniform reaction amongst Catholics to that Orange march.

This worsening, according to a man greatly respected as a negotiator between Orangemen and Catholic residents, is because when the bombings and shootings were common, the majority on 'both sides' transferred all culpability to the paramilitaries: if only they would stop, this would be a great wee place. And then they did stop. And the silent majority became vocal. And the voices were discordant.

The more we speak, the less we hear. The more we witness, the less we understand. We do not like them, and we like them less every day. This is the partition no amount of talking can unite. ❑

John O'Farrell, a native of Dublin, has been the editor of Fortnight *magazine in Belfast since 1995*

NOAM CHOMSKY

Serial veto

The Palestinian–Israeli 'peace process' can only be understood as a vindication of 50 years of force

IN NOVEMBER 1947, the UN General Assembly recommended that mandatory Palestine (cis-Jordan) be partitioned into Jewish and Palestinian states. The UN resolution was accepted by most of the Jewish community, and rejected by almost all Arabs. Civil strife broke out at once, with terror and violence on both sides. The better-organised Jewish community had the upper hand. By the time Israel declared its independence in May 1948, it incorporated parts of what was to be the Palestinian state and some 300,000 Arabs had fled or were expelled. Armies of the Arab states then entered the conflict. Subsequent fighting was mostly within the territory assigned to the Palestinian state, which was effectively divided between Israel and Transjordan (later Jordan), while the refugee flow more than doubled. Israel's internationally recognised borders are basically those of the 1949 cease-fire lines; Jordan's share ('the West Bank') gained little formal recognition. US policy had been ambivalent until May 1948, when Truman recognised the newly-founded Jewish state.

In 1956, Israel invaded Egypt together with France and Britain. The US opposed the action, and forced them to withdraw. In June 1967 Israel conquered the Gaza Strip and Sinai again, this time with US support, also taking over the West Bank and the Syrian Golan Heights. Several hundred thousand more refugees fled or were expelled.

In November 1967, the UN Security Council adopted Resolution 242 as the basis for diplomatic settlement. UN 242 called for peace between Israel and the Arab states in return for Israeli withdrawal from the territories occupied in the June war. The archival record remains largely closed, but enough has appeared to make it clear that Washington accepted – in fact, helped forge – the international consensus on full Israeli withdrawal, with at most marginal and mutual adjustments. That position was reiterated in the 1969 Rogers plan of the Nixon Administration.

UN 242 is strictly rejectionist. It accords no right of self-determination to one of the two contestants for national rights in the former Palestine. Palestinian rights are mentioned only in the reference to 'a just settlement of the refugee problem', left unspecified, on the tacit assumption that the refugees have the right of return or compensation that was endorsed unanimously by the General Assembly in December 1948 (Resolution 194). This was a direct application of Article 13 of the Universal Declaration of Human Rights (UDHR), adopted the day before. Resolution 194 has been reconfirmed regularly by the UN, with US agreement until December 1993, when the Clinton administration rejected it (along with Israel), effectively rescinding the resolution along with Article 13 of the UDHR; in the real world, a negative US vote amounts to a veto.

In 1967, the Arab states refused full peace and Israel refused full withdrawal, adopting instead the 1968 Allon Plan. Its basic principle is that Israel has a claim to the resources of the occupied territories and a good part of the usable land, but will take no responsibility for the Arab population, who are to be administered by Jordan or locally. Though particulars have changed over the years, the fundamental conception remains intact. The differences between the two major political groupings, Labour and Likud, have not been very large; the plan of the ultra-right General Ariel Sharon, for example, differs little from Labour's proposals of the same year (1992).

The impasse over UN 242 was broken in February 1971, when Egyptian President Sadat accepted the official US position, limiting himself to Israel-Egypt relations, a 'famous...milestone' on the path to peace, in the words of Yitzhak Rabin, then Israel's ambassador to Washington. Israel welcomed this officially as a genuine peace offer, but rejected it, stating that 'Israel will not withdraw to the pre-June 5 1967 borders.' The US had to decide whether to maintain its earlier policy, accepting Egypt as a client state and leaving Israel isolated, or to adopt Israel's preference for expansion (hence inevitable confrontation). The latter option was chosen, in accord with Henry Kissinger's call for 'stalemate': force, not diplomacy. Since then, the US has interpreted UN 242 as requiring only partial withdrawal – in effect, as determined by the US and Israel, which were almost alone in this stance.

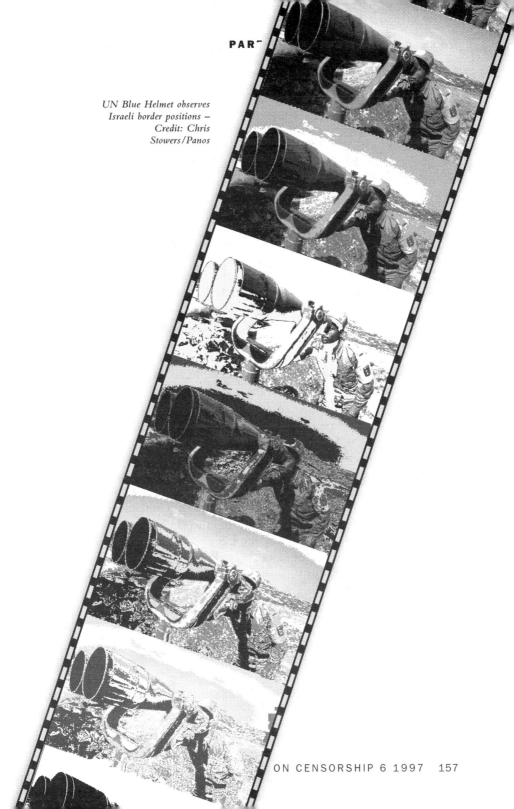

UN Blue Helmet observes
Israeli border positions –
Credit: Chris
Stowers/Panos

US isolation mounted in the mid-1970s as the international consensus shifted to a non-rejectionist settlement, incorporating the basic idea of partition, but now with a much smaller Palestinian state. In January 1976, the Security Council debated a resolution incorporating the wording of UN 242 and calling for a Palestinian state alongside Israel. The resolution was supported by virtually the entire world, including the Arab 'confrontation states' (Egypt, Syria, Jordan) and the Palestine Liberation Organisation (PLO), which 'prepared' the resolution, according to Israel's UN ambassador Haim Herzog (later president). Israel refused to attend the session. The US vetoed the resolution again in 1980.

After the rejection of his 1971 peace offer, Sadat appealed to Washington by expelling Soviet advisers and in other ways, but in vain. He also threatened war if diplomatic options were blocked. Despite many warnings to take these threats seriously, Washington dismissed them, adopting Israel's assumptions about its overwhelming military dominance.

The 1973 war dispelled these triumphalist attitudes. Recognising that Egypt could not simply be disregarded, US diplomacy moved to the next best option: to remove Egypt from the conflict. The policy culminated in the Camp David agreements of 1978-79. The US and Israel now accepted Sadat's 1971 proposals, while dismissing his new call for Palestinian rights. With the main Arab deterrent removed, Israel was free to integrate the occupied territories and attack Lebanon, with vastly increasing US aid. The consequences were implicit in the logic of the agreements, as is now often acknowledged.

Meanwhile the US continued to block diplomatic initiatives from the UN, Europe, the Arab states, the USSR and the PLO. Though the Security Council was eliminated by the US veto, the General Assembly continued to pass similar resolutions regularly with overwhelming support, US-Israel opposed. The last such vote was in December 1990 (144-2). None of these initiatives are considered to be part of the 'peace process,' for good reasons: they were opposed by the world's most powerful state, which has long insisted on controlling the Middle East, with its enormous energy resources.

By the late 1980s, US-Israeli rejectionism was facing difficulties. The Palestinian *Intifada* threatened Israel's control of the territories, and Washington was unable to sustain its posture of 'not hearing' the initiatives from the PLO and others. Various diplomatic manoeuvrings ensued. In reality, the parties maintained their positions with little change.

In December 1989, the Bush administration announced its terms for diplomatic settlement. This plan endorsed the 1989 proposals of Israel's Likud-Labour coalition (Yitzhak Shamir and Shimon Peres) as the sole basis for negotiations. The Shamir-Peres plan had two main provisions:
- there can be no 'additional Palestinian state' (Jordan already being a 'Palestinian state');
- the status of the occupied territories will be determined 'in accordance with the basic guidelines of the [Israeli] Government.'

There remained the problem of how to implement the rejectionist US-Israeli plan, which then had little international support. That problem was solved a few months later when Washington's ally and trading partner Saddam Hussein invaded Kuwait, having misunderstood the rules of world order, as dictators are prone to do. The outcome made it clear that at least in the Middle East, the US intended to run the show without interference. The US at once initiated a unilateral peace process on its own terms, at Madrid in 1991.

The next major step was in September 1993, when the Declaration of Principles (DOP) was signed in Washington by Prime Minister Rabin and Yasser Arafat. The DOP says little, but does have one important provision: that the 'permanent settlement' will be based on UN 242 alone, not supplemented with UN resolutions that recognise Palestinian rights. Furthermore, UN 242 is to be understood in US terms, hence as requiring only partial withdrawal. Details are spelled out in later agreements, notably the Oslo II agreement of September 1995. Oslo II completes the job of dismantling UN 242, even eliminating its central provision that rights cannot be gained by military conquest. On the contrary, the agreement stipulates that Palestinians 'shall respect the legal rights of Israelis (including corporations owned by Israelis)' throughout the occupied territories, including 'areas under the territorial jurisdiction of the [Palestinian] Council.' It also spells out conditions for the permanent settlement that guarantee Israeli control of the bulk of the West Bank's most valuable resource (water), along with restrictions on Palestinian travel and other matters. The Palestinian Authority meanwhile assumes all 'liabilities and obligations arising with regard to acts and omissions' of the military occupation, and 'shall immediately reimburse Israel the full amount' of any award for such practices.

After the signing of the DOP, the Rabin-Peres governments, with lavish US aid, rapidly expanded settlement and infrastructure programmes in the territories. The announced goal was to implement a version of the Allon plan, in particular, extending 'Greater Jerusalem' to the east, effectively dividing the West Bank into two separate cantons. A third Palestinian canton is in Gaza, where Israel is to keep about a third of the region along with much of its meagre water resources. Other infrastructure and settlement programmes subordinate further the areas to be left to local Palestinian administration under Israeli control. The final settlement dismisses the 'refugee problem,' which 'is, and has always been, the heart of the conflict' (Danny Rubinstein, who covered the territories for leading Israeli journals with great distinction).

In its design and execution, the US-forged peace process resembles South Africa's Bantustan programme, with the Palestinian Authority playing the role of the Black elites who were to control the population in these 'independent states,' under South African supervision, brutally if need be and with ample opportunities for self-enrichment – a role quickly adopted by Arafat and his entourage. South Africa's Homelands policy, however, did not qualify as a 'peace process,' again, for the simple and sufficient reason that it was not implemented by the dominant global power.

It is commonly held that the 'peace process' broke down because of the extremism of the Netanyahu (Likud) government, crucially, its decision to construct 6,500 housing units for Jews only in southeast Jerusalem (Israel's 'Har Homa'). In this as in most other respects, however, Netanyahu is carrying out Labour government plans; the execution is sometimes more harsh than Labour's practices, sometimes less so. The Har Homa project, in particular, was announced by the Peres government in February 1996; preparations on the ground were underway before Netanyahu was elected. Furthermore, other projects announced by Labour at the same time, now also being implemented by Likud, are – rather plausibly – considered by Israeli hawks to be more important, notably the plans to link the Jerusalem region to Israel's expanding urban settlements to the east, another project fostered by the Rabin-Peres Labour governments. The crucial difference between Labour and Likud programmes was noted by the Housing Minister of the Peres government, who announced these projects: Labour 'does everything quietly,' he explained, not in the brazen style of Likud. The programmes are similar, but Labour's manner of execution is more attuned to western sensibilities.

The 'peace process' should, I think, be understood as an impressive vindication of the rule of force in international affairs, at both policy and doctrinal levels: the former, by virtue of its operative significance, the latter, in the light of the broad acceptance of the rejectionist stance that Washington had maintained in virtual isolation for many years. However one evaluates the outcome, much pain and suffering surely lie ahead. ❏

Noam Chomsky is a professor in the Department of Linguistics and Philosophy at the Massachusetts Institute of Technology in Cambridge, Mass. His latest works include Language and Thought *(1994),* Powers and Prospects *(1996) and* Class Warfare *(1996)*

West Bank demonstrator during the Intifada – Credit: JC Tordai/Panos

ERIC WATKINS

Still looking for unity

The contest in Yemen is rigged – but the game goes on

O N 22 May 1990, the Yemen Arab Republic in the north and the People's
Democratic Republic of Yemen in the south of that divided land united
to form the Republic of Yemen, a new state dedicated to democratic reform
and economic liberalisation. By 1994, the North, with roughly three times
the population of the South, was at war with its tiny neighbour. The victory
of the North under its President General Ali Abdullah Saleh ensured unity
was preserved but at a price.

Human rights organisations have noted the cost. 'The government of Ali
Abdullah Saleh, which prevailed in Yemen's civil war, further constricted civil
and political rights in that country,' says Human Rights Watch's 1997 *World
Report*, adding, 'in 1996 Yemen's human rights profile compared unfavourably
with the relative tolerance that had characterised the four years following the
May 1990 unification.'

What went wrong? The unification of the two Yemens was hasty. As the
lone Marxist state in the Middle East, South Yemen had been dependent on
Soviet support since 1967. The collapse of the Soviet Union left the South
and its leaders exposed. From their standpoint, union with the North meant a
new lease of life, enabling them to retain their leadership in a transitional government following unification and, possibly, to rule after the proposed elections.

Northern leaders also had their reasons for the merger. Since worker
remittances from the Gulf, a mainstay of the economy, had begun to fall in the
early eighties, the North had its own economic problems. The discovery of oil
in 1984 promised new revenues and production started in 1987. By 1990,
however, the modest income generated was already in decline and suspected

new reserves straddled the border with the South. Joint exploitation following unification was the only way either side could enjoy the potential wealth.

Unification was heralded with a fanfare of political freedom: a liberal press law was passed, some 100 press licences were granted and a plethora of information hit the streets. Then came the Gulf War and Yemen was hit hard: the country's ambiguous stance, condemning both the Iraqi invasion of Kuwait *and* the US-led coalition, led the Gulf states to cut aid and expel nearly one million Yemeni workers and their families. The impact of the returnees and the loss of their remittances devastated the economy, sending the exchange rate down and inflation up. Faced with popular discontent, the coalition government began to unravel. Amid growing acrimony between the two leaders, northern President Ali Abdullah Saleh and southern Vice-President Ali Salem al-Biedh, elections scheduled for November 1992 were postponed until April 1993.

The 1993 elections split the coalition even further. Although Saleh and al-Biedh had agreed to run the country jointly after the elections, Saleh chose to honour a similar pre-election agreement with the fundamentalist Islah party to the detriment of al-Beidh. Increasingly marginalised by the new coalition partners after the elections, al-Biedh retired to Aden in June 1993. His continued absence over the next 11 months fuelled his dispute with Saleh; by 1994, military clashes across the old border had escalated into full-blown civil war.

Post-war Yemen has not fared well. National elections, held in April 1997, were boycotted by major opposition parties because of government control of the broadcast media – crucial in a country where 60 per cent of the population cannot read – and because of voter registration fraud. Saleh was declared the winner, but the opposition was eliminated. 'In the long term,' as Brian Whitaker, author of *National Unity and Democracy in Yemen* has noted, 'the lack of effective and credible opposition cannot be healthy: democracy is a game for more than one player.'

Nevertheless, the game continues. Mohammed al-Mutawakil, an opposition leader, explains the rules: 'The ideological confrontation in our country is not a confrontation between capitalism and Marxism or between nationalism and regionalism or between Muslims and non-believers or between South and North. It is a confrontation between a democratic ideology and an oppressive ideology.' ❏

Eric Watkins is a London-based journalist specialising in Middle Eastern and Central Asian affairs.

VERA RICH

Grave matters

A quarrel over the dead has exhumed the 'floozy of history' in the Eastern Marches

POLAND is the classic example of partition in its most extreme form. Having disappeared from the map of Europe in the eighteenth century, after drastic 'surgery' by its neighbours – Russia, Austria and Prussia – Poland reappeared against all odds as a state after World War I. Ironically, this included a broad band of territory – known to the Poles as the Kresy Schódne (Eastern Marches) – partitioned off from the ethnic homelands of its eastern neighbours, the Lithuanians, Belarusians and Ukrainians. After World War II, Poland was, in Churchill's words, 'moved westwards', losing the Kresy Schódne to the Soviet Union, and gaining a tranche of territory in the west. The effects of such frontier changes linger and, even today, can cause friction.

The roots of these disputes go back centuries: to the dynastic union, in 1386, of Poland and the multi-ethnic Grand Duchy of Lithuania-Rus-Samogitia, which incorporated today's Lithuania, Belarus and much of Ukraine. This, and the political union which followed in 1569, resulted in the formation of a broad swathe of territory with a mixed population. It is now impossible to draw a clear-cut ethnic boundary, with Poles tidily to the west and Lithuanians, Belarusians and Ukrainians to the east. All one can do is guarantee the ethnic communities stranded on the 'wrong' side of the frontier the cultural rights laid down in the international covenants on national minorities, defined in this context as coherent ethnic groups with a separate linguistic/cultural/religious identity which have been present in the territory in question for at least 100 years.

Poland has signed agreements with its three newly independent eastern neighbours, Lithuania, Belarus and Ukraine, on mutual assurances of respect for their respective national minorities. Implementing these guarantees is, however, another matter; from time to time there have been bizarre incidents that become headline news on the other side of the frontier.

Such a row flared up in June this year, over a cemetery in Ukraine's second city Lviv (Lwów to the Poles). During the Polish-Ukrainian conflict of 1918-19, there had been major action around the city, in the course of which many members of a Polish youth unit were killed. After the area was allotted to Poland in 1923, the cemetery where these 'Eaglets' were interred became a Polish patriotic shrine. When the Soviets took over the area in the post World War II settlements, the cemetery, like many other monuments of Polish rule, was destroyed: a road was built across it, and part of what was left became a municipal graveyard. Now the local Poles want to reconstruct and reconsecrate the 'Eaglets' cemetery'. The Lviv city council duly gave their consent, and renovation started. However, Polish plans included restoring the original inscriptions, which spoke of the Eaglets as having laid down their lives in defence of Lwów and Kresy Schódne.

This outraged Ukrainian feeling. If the Eaglets were 'defending' the city and its environs, they protested, then the Poles were implying that the Ukrainians were invaders. City council and the cemetery management ordered the controversial plaques removed. While the Poles argued that they had simply replaced the inscriptions destroyed by the Soviets, Ukrainians claimed the wording was a new provocation. The row escalated with some Poles suggesting that the Ukrainians wanted to destroy the cemetery completely. 'No way,' said Mayor Vasyl Kuykida of Lviv, pledging he would do all in his power to assist reconstruction – providing, of course, that the Poles gave up their provocative inscriptions.

The row now went top-level. Poland's Defence Minister, Stanislaw Dobrzanski, on a two-day visit to Kyiv to discuss closer military co-operation, took time out to discuss the cemetery issue with Ukrainian foreign minister Hennadiy Udovenko. Polish Foreign Minister Dariusz Rosaiti said that it was all doubtless 'a misunderstanding', and President Aleksander Kwasniewski despatched one of his senior advisers to Lviv on a 'goodwill mission' to try to sort things out.

After five hours of heavy negotiating, a Polish-Ukrainian protocol was signed, permitting restoration of the Eaglets' cemetery to go ahead within the current boundaries of the graveyard. The 300-odd graves outside the present wall would be exhumed, and the Eaglets reinterred within. The Poles would submit detailed plans for Ukrainian approval. It was, however, implicitly accepted that the controversial inscriptions would be dropped.

'Would this not be a falsification of history?' a Polish reporter asked the mayor of Lviv. 'History,' he replied, 'is like a woman of light morals. Anyone can get her into bed. We don't need to spend time gossiping about such a floozy. What we need now is mutual understanding!' ❏

Vera Rich is a freelance journalist

The Brandenburg Gate following the fall of theBerlin Wall, 1989 Credit: Rex

WL WEBB

Notes from Dunkeldeutschland

Reunification turns out to have a rather different price tag from the one west Germans thought worth paying for at the time. The hidden cost is now falling due and it's the '*Ossis*' – east Germans – who are paying with post-dated credits. And for many, the 'disappearing' of their past is too heavy a price.

'THE past is a foreign country...' Perhaps *this* is the clue to a persisting distinct identity in what west German schoolboys call '*Dunkeldeutschland*', dark Germany. For here it is: the collective German past, eerily preserved in so much of the eastern provinces, with their cobbled streets and stretches of two-lane Nazi-time autobahn; haunting the quiet villages of Brandenburg and Mecklenburg-Vorpommern, and the rotting plaster of old apartment blocks in the uncolonised parts of east Berlin and other large cities, the *Mietzkaserne*, 'rent-barracks', of the 1920s, updated only by bullet scars from the great Russian offensive that determined the fate of East Germany for nearly half a century.

In November 1989, I drove north to Berlin with the shouts of that extraordinary Leipzig crowd, like some vast opera chorus, ringing in my ears; already it was making the profoundly significant modulations from '*Wir sind das Volk*' – We are the people – to *Wir sind* ein *Volk* – We are one nation – and then, Germany, one Fatherland!

Preoccupied as I was with history in the making, I couldn't help realising that almost all the way from Wittenberg to Potsdam an old, cobbled, arrow-straight Prussian military road was unrolling in my headlights through the snow. This autumn, when I drove back down from

Berlin, that road was closed, but the rambling deviation administered the same jarring history lesson. And at night, Luther's little city still looked lost in a time-warp, somewhere between the Renaissance and the eve of Hitler's seizure of power.

Once you leave behind central-east Berlin's vast building sites, or redeveloping Dresden, Halle and Leipzig, the otherness you experience is first of all this sense of time-travelling into the collective German past. But there is also the other half of LP Hartley's famous sentence: 'The past is a foreign country: they do things differently there.'

For of course the late and, as a political system unlamented, German Democratic Republic, didn't only preserve large parts of the German heritage shabbily intact. As well as building the blood-stained Wall, more to keep people in than keep them out, it also stamped the old landscape with the structures of the industrial proletarian culture of its dreams. The wreck of those dreams you can see in closed factories outside small towns all over the eastern Länder, but most dramatically in the vast lunar landscapes of abandoned open-cast mines in Saxon-Anhalt, in the miles of filthy ghost factories girdling Bitterfeld, the industrial town north of Leipzig that was the centre of the German chemical industry. (And will be again: gleaming strangely here and there amid the dereliction are the newly built hi-tech outposts of multinationals like Bayer, employing, however, far fewer of the skilled local workforce.) And after a while, beyond the shiny new cars and shopfronts, through the chaos of cranes and concrete at the once and future Potsdamer Platz, you begin to see something of the wreckage of people's lives in the upheaval of unification.

Somewhere suspended between these two pasts, of the GDR and of an older Germany, is a large part of the identity of the Germans of 'the new Länder'. Quite what this is is not easy for them to say. Do they think they are just Germans, or perhaps Saxons, or Brandenburgers? Are they the second-class citizens of a kind of Deutschland B, as comparative statistics suggest? Or perhaps another kind of German, more authentic, traditional, unamericanized...? You get nearer the heart of the matter when, like them, you ask yourself what they are supposed to do with their own self-histories from the years before the great change.

For what they feel they are being told – by Bonn, by the political and economic culture which has flooded their lives since 1990, by those they

call the *Besserwessis*, the *Wessis* who always know better – is simple: forget it; it was all an aberration, all of it. We know better, not only about
our own way of life, but about yours too; and our way's the only way.
Join the real world. (A cigarette widely advertised in the east is called
West: 'West – the power of now!')

If this were the whole, simple truth, it would still be a case of easier
said than done. But now the excitement of being let loose in the fun fair
of consumerism is past, and the cost of the spree much clearer, what they
are being told to think about their lives before 'The Change' strikes not
a few of them as yet another kind of censorship. (So, incidentally, does
the western takeover of the *Berliner Zeitung*, the 'non-party' paper which
east Berliners had thought of as their own. The eastern identity lacks
media voices of its own, a need which a reformed *Neues Deutschland*
under the aegis of the post-Communist Social Democratic party (PDS)
scarcely satisfies.) This is not the least important of the second, third and
fourth thoughts about unification and how it was done, that have caused
the *Ossis*'s widely observed 'drawing back'.

How curious easterners working in west Berlin were about everything at first, how keen to meet people, join things, shop there. 'Now
that's all over,' I'm told: 'they just go back to their own neighbourhoods
in the east.' And the *Ossis* are not just shopping near home; they have
gone back massively to buying the old, once despised, GDR brand products, like 'Club' Cola, advertised now with: 'Hooray, I'm still alive! Club
Cola, our Cola!' Or Bürger Knäcke – east Germany's favourite crisp-
bread – 'a crispy bit of *Heimat*!' Realising that west Berliners too had
been losers – of the tax concessions, low rents, exemption from military
service once bestowed on the beleaguered Free World bastion – hadn't
brought them closer again. Of the city's 16,383 weddings last year, only
562 were between east and west Berliners.

Statistics crudely outline the scale of the changes they have gone
through. One fifth of Germany's population, the east has a third of its
unemployment: the official rate veers between 17 per cent and 20 per
cent, but when you take into account extensive early retirement, retraining and make-work programmes, the reality is far worse. All this, of
course, among people to whom for more than 40 years, unemployment
was unknown, whatever the quality or economic viability of some of the
jobs.

As for the vast privatisation operation, estimates published in *Die Woche*, show that 85 per cent of east Germany's industries are now owned by west Germans, 10 per cent by foreign owners; only five per cent remain in east German hands. Only 4.1 per cent of German spending on research goes east, and production there has still not recovered to the level of 1989. Thomas Mayer, chief economist in Frankfurt for Goldman Sachs, is quoted as saying, 'Nobody invests in the east to make profits, but to get subsidies.' Certainly, the transfer of ownership has involved, as well as subsidy-farming and asset stripping, massive closures of industrial plant – sometimes with great environmental benefit, though not all were dinosaurs – and a ruthless stripping out of industrial jobs.

For the rest, you had to get rid of the vast, corrupting Stasi apparatus, reform the police and the legal profession (much more thoroughly than was done after the collapse of Nazism – in many law faculties all the professors were fired), and replace the ranks of teachers of sclerotic 'Marxism-Leninism' with specialists in disciplines essential to a capitalist economy that scarcely existed in the GDR. The extent of the purge in the universities, nevertheless, hints at the scale of the shakeup the socialist 'middle class' went through. More than a third of the staff of institutes of higher education had gone by 1995, and only 35 per cent of professors who had taught in the humanities are still in their chairs, while 20 per cent of the total remain unfilled.

Some changes combined the 'cultural' and ideological. 'Medical faculties in East Germany, to take only the most well known – the Charité in Berlin and Jena – were characterised by their excellent teaching and very 'human atmosphere'', wrote Martin Berger, an *Ossi* student, in a recent number of *Daedalus*. 'Reunification imposed the western kind of numerically-orientated medical teaching procedures in our excellent faculties. They became less 'human' unwillingly. This is one of the sacrifices of unification.' New hi-tech equipment didn't altogether compensate for this sense of loss.

Some snapshots from lives lived through the change: Maraike (the middle of three generations I was to meet of a family of impressive women who grew up under Communism) described her traverse from working happily before the change in the former children's radio drama department, another of the GDR's acknowledged centres of excellence, to doing counselling, after retraining as a family therapist. She is obviously good at this too, though she suffers for and with the young women who come to her office in Marzahn, where many young families grapple with the deprivations of unemployment.

Women have done particularly badly in the downsizing economy. A large and crucial part of the workforce under Communism, they are now the largest part of the unemployment figures. In Brandenburg, for example, where 92 per cent of women used to have jobs, they are 65 per cent of the out of work. With the work went crêches, and a package which gave a year's maternity leave and kept the job open for up to three years. Unsurprisingly, many women, especially single women with children, are left feeling isolated, unsupported by either the companionship of work or social arrangements which didn't make bringing up children such a lonely solo performance. From this flow other statistics, like the astonishing halving of the birthrate in the eastern lands since 1989. More sinister, if *Der Spiegel* is to be believed, is the rise in cases of young women so desperate to get jobs that they are having themselves sterilised.

Some of the strangest things Maraike tells me about her new situation slip out almost parenthetically. She works side by side with other professionals who are west Berliners. Some, though not all, are more experienced, but all have much the same qualifications. Yet all the easterners are deemed to be five years 'younger' for purposes of increments, pensions and so forth. Even stranger, though basic salary levels are now similar, the *Ossis* work a 40-hour-week, but the *Wessis* only 38.5 hours. The same arrangements, she tells me, hold for nearly everyone in public service jobs, a strangely ritual, hierarchical reinforcement of the sense of difference.

As with many others, especially in and around Berlin, the house in which she has lived is suddenly owned by someone else; in Potsdam alone, there have been 5,000 claims by, usually, the descendants of dispossessed westerners. In Maraike's case the west German claimant was trumped by a claim from the Jewish Claims Conference agency on behalf of previous Jewish owners dispossessed in the time of the Nazis, and now Maraike pays her rent to a local office of the agency.

'Strange' is a word often used by people I talk to. Maraike's vivid young daughter Anna, who has just made a funny, shrewd little film which she hopes will win her a place at film school, takes me to see *Wittstock, Wittstock* a remarkable feature-length documentary by Voelker Koepp. Begun under the GDR, it follows the fate of women who were the workforce in a textile factory in a little, time-warped Brandenburg town, from the early 1970s – stroppy and confident in their work and companionship, telling the (male) management just what's wrong with their organisation and equipment – through the baffling insecurities which quickly follow the takeover by a western firm, up to the present day. Now nearly everyone's out of work, the film's natural star on her fourth 'retraining' programme and still no job. 'It's not normal,' says her mate, once forewoman in charge of hundreds. 'Before, everyone had work and did something in their lives.'

Wittstock, Wittstock could tell Bonn's politicians and social engineers more about how it is in the east than yards of statistics. It is, of course, showing only in a small cinema in an outer suburb of east Berlin.

Maraike, Anna and Urszula her grandmother, aren't whingers or constitutional nostalgics. All of them, better equipped to adapt than their Wittstock sisters, are getting on with life. Urszula, an agricultural scientist in her late 60s, widow of the brilliant and stubbornly Communist journalist Alan Winnington, now runs an Aladdin's cave of a shop in Prenzlauer Berg, which Anna helped her to set up, selling jewel-coloured Asian textiles and other things that are still new treasure there. But even Anna, who finished her schooling under the new order, is likely to go on feeling it very odd that *individuals*, not the community, should own whole apartment blocks or chunks of the countryside. Maraike says: 'I think Anna likes her childhood, and doesn't feel ashamed of her parents' lives.'

Many people share such feelings, in spite of the moral and psychological havoc wreaked by the Stasi and their files, and the enthusiastic exploitation of the files in the war on the past that has accompanied unification. More than that, they feel that with the new gains in political freedom and consumer choice, there are also things of value they have lost from that other time in the other country. This too is not easy to describe. The young wife of an English craftsman who has settled in the half-restored Cranach Hof in Wittenberg, had several shy attempts before settling on one of those resounding German portmanteau words: '*Zusammengehörigkeitsgefühl*. That's what it was, people had this, well, feeling-of-belonging-together.' With it, even in Wittenberg but far more in bigger places, had somehow gone the time for such intimacy and availability, gone in the new hard-driven economy, with its cars and 'handy' phones that too many people had bought on tick before realising they were going to lose their jobs. Going fast, too, was a kind of ingenuity at fixing things that went with the culture of scarcity, and the companionableness of swapping skills and useful bits and pieces.

Is what has been happening here simply a speeded up version of the uncomfortable journey people have been making everywhere from South Wales to Clydeside and across the US rustbowl: that journey from the past to the future, to a largely de-industrialised world built around a volatile and depoliticized consumerism, where old solidarities and modest securities have disappeared with the old workplaces, and economic indiscipline is punished by politically unaccountable global markets? Or could east Germany be a kind of test case, a place where neo-liberalism's assumptions about what life and work and politics are for are challenged not by theory but by the different experience of a population which, ironically, protected itself from a harsh and deformed ideology by adapting for its own needs Communism's old ideals of equality and fraternity?

It's not that the *Ossis* don't appreciate much of what arrived with unification: from the freedom to vote and travel to reliable cars and modern electronics for those who can afford them, and a touch of class in the clothes they wear. But couldn't 'They', over there, have imagined that they too might have *something* to learn from what we had done during those 40-odd years? If not from a transport system that pushed goods traffic off the roads and on to the railways, then from our simpler, more directly democratic way of talking and living with one another? Something that had little to do with the Party's 'proletarian' style, and penetrated deeply into work and relationships, so that, for example, marriages and parenting between a dentist and a bricklayer, a doctor and a joiner, unimaginable in the west, weren't especially unusual.

Certainly the fierceness of the criticism in some west German papers and magazines of this kind of thinking ('deluded nostalgia'), and the ideological intensity of the *Literaturstreit* over the body of east German writing ('phoney moralisers!'), suggests that something serious is at issue here; as did outrage at the opposition of Günter Grass and other left-wing west German writers to the way unification was done. 'Our capitalists and Communists have always had one thing in common,' wrote Grass. 'They condemn the Third Way out of hand.'

Even where there is good will and no particular suspicion, the causes of mutual misunderstanding are many and complicated. Easterners, childlike in this as in their great early shopping spree, had to learn how to read the rhetoric of the new system which was to be so unlike the manipulative dishonesty of what they had rejected. For a while, they were at a loss in the gap between new rhetoric and new reality. Now they're catching on.

Christoph Hein, the notably unsentimental east German novelist and playwright, much censored himself under the old order, was a cautionary voice amid the early euphoria. The process of coming together for east and west, he said then, would take as long as the time they had spent apart. 'Today,' he told *Die Zeit* recently, 'I think it will take longer. At the end of 1990, people were correcting themselves, if they used the

At the Berlin Wall, 1989: chipping away at the past – Credit: Rex

expression GDR, and saying "east Germany, the new Bundesländer".
Now they talk much more readily of the GDR. Among west Germans,
there's increasingly a lack of interest, while the interest of the east
Germans in the west, almost laughably intense in '89-'90, has turned
into total uninterest.'

Or, as the Erfurt Declaration (a new blast against the achievements of
the Kohl government, signed by Grass and Friedrich Schorlemmer,
among others) puts it: 'Many people in the new Bundesländer experience what is currently happening as expropriating the rights they had
earned as well as their hopes of freedom, equality and human fellow-
feeling. In the west, many think they are giving everything to the east;
there, many think every last thing is being taken from them.'

Meanwhile, a headline in *Tageszeitung,* the west Berlin leftist paper,
says, 'Friedrichstrasse with all its posh new post-Wall shops is dead as a
doornail, while in the west the old Kurfürstendamm is booming.' The
money isn't flowing east as hoped. Investors have pulled out, the
grandiose Checkpoint Charlie project has collapsed, builders are being
laid off. The great tangled cranes begin to look like giant question
marks: When the government does finally move from Bonn to Berlin
can even that manage to shift the focus of the country's life eastwards?
And then, the history of this place being what it is, a still bigger question
looms: What might rise up from the unsettled German past if the global
market, spinning ever more madly, one day knocks the new world order
flat on its face?

W L Webb, formerly literary editor of the Guardian, *is now a freelance writer
with a particular interest in post-Communist Central Europe*

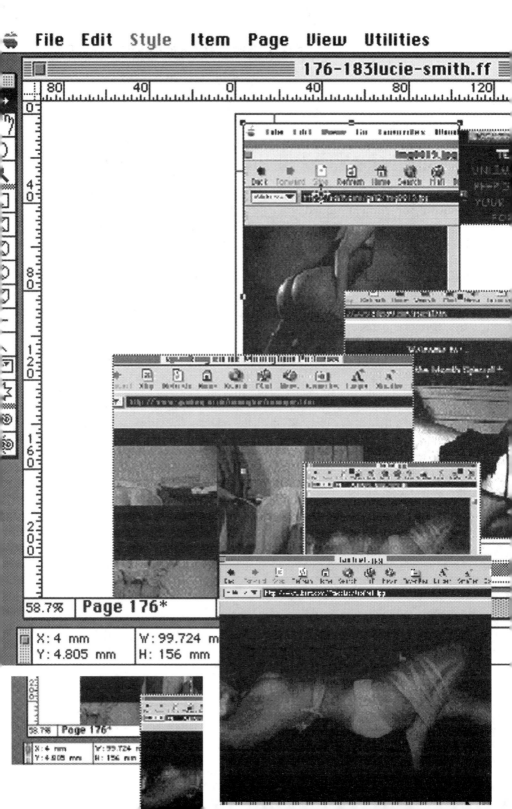

EDWARD LUCIE-SMITH

Bodies of evidence

THE Internet has become part of people's lives with astonishing rapidity. What was essentially an amusement for techno-freaks, three years ago, and a pretty frustrating one at that, with agonisingly slow download times and frequent technical glitches, has now taken its place in almost everyone's awareness. Tony Blair embraces Bill Gates of Microsoft, whom computers have made into far and away the world's richest man, and together they vow to bring the Internet into every British classroom. When Diana, Princess of Wales was killed in a motor accident in Paris, over 300,000 people queued to sign the condolence books which were opened at St James's Palace, and which were later moved to Kensington Palace. At the same time, however, 540,000 people signed the 'virtual' condolence book which was opened on the Internet. Many newspapers now publish regular Internet supplements. Some, like *Le Monde* in France, run an Internet page every day. The journalistic motto is, if you can't beat them, join them. Every major news publishing and news gathering organisation now has its own Internet site. If you can't be bothered to stick with CNN on television till you reach the part of the news cycle which happens to interest you, boot your computer and get Netscape to transport you to cnn.com. One mouse-click will take you to the relevant topic.

The concerns which were very recently being voiced about Internet content have for the moment faded from public awareness, but they will undoubtedly return. Even as I write, obscure committees of high-powered civil servants are meeting in back rooms, here in Europe and also in the United States, looking for ways to 'regulate the Net', either by means of new laws, or, better still, through the introduction of technological locks, bars and handcuffs. And quite a few non-official persons are also worrying about what you can find on it. Basically the areas of concern can be split into three categories: pornography, authenticity and copyright. Of these pornography has made by far the most noise. It is also, at least superficially, the one which seems closest to the concerns of *Index on Censorship*.

There is no doubt that a great deal of Internet content is erotic. This applies particularly to images as opposed to text. New, superfast modems benefit images particularly. One picture of relatively modest size – half the area of the average computer screen – demands as many computer bytes as a text of perhaps ten thousand words. A short video-clip will need as many bytes as a very long novel. There are erotic sites and home-pages all over the Net. Some are entirely free. Some are in principle free, but demand some kind of ID from the viewer, who has to pay a small sum to obtain it. One of the most popular of these identification systems is AdultCheck, which combines the first four digits of the applicant's credit card with a 'secret' password chosen by himself or herself. The idea is that no-one under 18 can get hold of the requisite piece of plastic (and if you'll believe that you'll believe anything). Others still are pay-per-view. The free erotic sites very generally support themselves by including advertisements for the commercial ones – plus a 'link' which will take you right to the spot.

In a sense, however, to make a fuss about any of these sites is irrelevant. The prime sources for erotica on the Net are not the various erotic pages you may stumble across using a browser, but the news groups, which can be reached without using anything as elaborate as Netscape or Microsoft Explorer. All you need is a simple programme like Newswatcher. There are over twenty thousand news groups currently available on the net, and they cater for every conceivable interest and every possible sexual taste. Fantasies about castration? Then click on 'alt. eunuchs. questions'. This is a relatively small news group. On any given day you will probably find just short of 200 items, or 'articles': pictures, fiction, reminiscences, queries about where to get the job done for real.

The erotic pictures appear for the most part under the heading 'alt.binaries'. There are a truly enormous number of them. There is a subscription Internet site called PictureView, which exists simply to bring together all the images which have appeared in the news groups over the past ten days. It offered, when I sneaked a quick look while writing this, '278,808 pictures in 371 groups'. More than 95% of these will be erotic, and categories range from 'alt.amazon.women' to 'alt.sex.necrophilia'. The server is automated, and the only things which those in charge of it attempt to weed out are pedophile images. Users are asked to report these when they encounter them. In the circumstances, you cannot blame even the relatively unpuritanical for becoming uneasy, and seeking ways to tame the flood.

However, this is a lot easier said than done. Late last June, for example, the US Supreme Court, by a 7-2 majority, struck down a central provision of the 1996 Communications Decency Act, which attempted to ban distribution of sexually explicit material to anyone under the age of 18. The act, sponsored by President Clinton, was specifically aimed at what was happening in cyberspace. Under the proposed law, it became a crime to put adult-orientated or "patently offensive" material on-line where children might find it. Both Internet providers and civil rights activists claimed that it would be technically impossible to impose effective censorship on the World Wide Web. But these were not the grounds for the Court's decision, which was based instead on the First Amendment right to free speech.

Any close examination of the erotic binaries on offer in the news groups shows that the vast majority originate in America. It shows a number of other things as well. One is that these erotic pictures have strangely mixed origins. Some come from the commercial peddlers of porn, and are samples of the merchandise they have on offer. Greatly to the irritation of many newsgroup aficionados, these merchants go in for the practice of 'spamming', posting the same binary files again and again. The same picture will be posted to a single group – often not even a relevant one – as many as a dozen times in a single day. The rest of the material comes from amateurs, often acting with blithe disregard for copyright. Thanks to the advent of cheap scanners – you can now buy an adequate scanner for less than £200 – any set of erotic pictures which happens some-one's fancy can easily make its way into the newsgroups. New issues of gay magazines like Honcho and Advocate Men are rapidly stripped of their picture spreads. Ancient porn, going as far back as the late 1960s and early 1970s, is hauled out of storage in the garage and put into circulation again. Certain favourite images, and sequences of images are now on their way to becoming immortal: they turn up again and again.

The success of the digital camera – the market for these is said to be growing by six hundred per cent per annum – has made a recent significant contribution to amount of erotica available on the Web. Sociologists seem to have underrated the exhibitionist element in contemporary society – on some days it seems as if every Tom, Dick and Tracey is busy putting saucy pictures of themselves on the Internet. These pictures are fascinating in more than one way, not merely for what they show so graphically, but for the immense divide in attitudes which they reveal between the rulers and the ruled.

Once an erotic image makes its way into cyberspace, it takes on an elusive and chameleon-like existence. It can be reposted at any time, sometimes cropped or otherwise altered, by anyone who happens to download it, anywhere in the world. And it need not carry the file-name it started out with.

The favourite pictures I have just mentioned appear under scores of different aliases – which makes their true origin almost impossible to trace. The same comment applies to erotic texts, and these are often much more brutally offensive than the pictures. It takes a thick skin to read some of the material posted to the Internet as erotic fiction. But then it also takes a thick skin to read the Marquis de Sade, whom the French have decided is a classic of their literature.

What the availability of this mass of erotic material really demonstrates, however, is that censorship has finally been vanquished by technology. In sophisticated western societies at least, we are witnessing the final stage of a process which began with Gutenberg, where the means of suppression always ran snapping at the heels of the means of dissemination. Today no law, no encryptment programme, no sort of social sanction can finally defeat a determined computer hacker. Much more important than this, no group of civil servants in a back room, no uprising of the religious right, no caucus of liberal do-gooders in rebellion against the consequences of their own ideology can get the better of the prolix, complex, multifarious, unimaginably profuse flow of information which has invaded cyberspace, or of the radical democratisation of the means of distributing that information which the personal computer has brought about.

This brings me to the two other issues which I mentioned at the beginning of this article – authenticity and copyright. To me they seem much more important than the question of eroticism. The Internet often attracts criticism from new users that information on a specific theme is not only hard to find, but, when found, turns out to be 'garbage'. In effect, the World Wide Web resounds with the noise of axes being ground. Every major world event brings with it is own crop of conspiracy theories, and these find immediate expression on the Internet. The Princess's fatal car-crash, for example, spawned a rash of 'alt.diana.conspiracy' newsgroups, each interpretation seeking to outdo its predecessors in terms of paranoia. The Internet has also provided fertile ground for the kind of libels which even the most reckless would hesitate to venture in traditional print, or even on the radio or on television. This August, official Washington was suddenly up in arms when a much-read Internet gossip column called the *Drudge Report* accused a Clinton aide of wife-beating. It was a step too far: the 'scoop' couldn't be substantiated, and people who had relished the other innuendoes in the column were suddenly embarrassed and ashamed. More to the point, they realised how vulnerable they themselves were to this kind of 'information'.

The nature of computer texts – and for that matter of computer images – their spontaneity and malleability, leads to a new conception of 'truth', rather similar to the view of historical accuracy enshrined in Hollywood director Oliver Stone's films JFK and Nixon. If it wasn't that way, then it should have been, and anyway it's what people prefer to believe. Anyone who attempts to substitute the correct version is regarded as a censor.

Net aficionados tend to treat those who try to defend copyright material from indiscriminate copying on the Web as censors almost worse than those who attempt to rid cyberspace of eroticism. For them, any defence of intellectual property rights is a form of theft. In fact the two issues – copyright and eroticism – are intimately linked. As I have already suggested, the creators of commercial pornography are amongst the most conspicuous victims of net piracy, and the amateurs who post these 'borrowed' images to the news groups must be costing the porn industry millions of dollars. However, pornographers are not the only victims. The witty British poet Wendy Cope recently launched a tirade – and a new poem – against those who put her work on the Internet without permission and without paying for it. Interestingly enough, educational institutions are amongst the worst offenders. A search based on Cope's name, made while I was writing this, immediately turned up a pirated version of Cope's popular poem '*Valentine*', on a site which belongs to an American school. For schools and colleges, putting a poem up on a web-site accessible to their students – but also to everyone else in the world with an Internet account – is only an extension of the long-hallowed practice of dishing out duplicated or xeroxed copies of material which is to be discussed in class.

While big corporations like Disney, already very tough about the protection of their copyrights, will undoubtedly institute legal action against some offenders, the likelihood is that the vast majority of net pirates will continue to get away with it – and most of them won't even be aware that they have broken the law. The wonderful world of cyberspace is likely to be the theatre of a major conflict of interest between those who create and those who consume. And the creators, perhaps to their horror, will find themselves on the side of what many web-users will call censorship. ❏

Edward Lucie-Smith is a well known art critic. His latest book is Ars Erotica *(1997)*

Look, Europe!

A message in a bottle

The case of Iranian editor Faraj Sarkoohi, which *Index* has monitored over the past year, inspired *Look, Europe!* - a play by banned Iranian writer Ghazi Rabihavi, whose work we have also featured. Harold Pinter, who met Ghazi Rabihavi at *Index's* banned fiction reading last year, presented a rehearsed reading of the play at the Almeida Theatre on 5 October as a

David MacCreedy & Harold Pinter –
Credit: Carlos Reyes-Manzo/Andes

benefit for Writers & Scholars Educational Trust, *Index's* associated charity.

Roger Lloyd Pack appeared as Sarkoohi who, in the course of the play, undergoes arrest and torture and, during a brief period of freedom, passes a letter describing his experiences to a tramp in a Tehran park. The tramp (played by Pinter, delivering gnomic utterances with manic energy), places the letter in a bottle, promising to make it public if Sarkoohi is rearrested.

The entire cast – Joseph Bennett, Anna Friel, Rhydian Jones, Andrew Lincoln, David MacCreedy, Nadia Sawalha, Nedim Sawalha, Christopher Simon and Malcolm Tierney – all gave their time free, as did director Gari Jones, assistant director Lotte Buchan and stage manager Sara Crosdale.

Index would like to thank them all for giving their time to this project. Their commitment was evident in the strength of the production which resulted. Our thanks too to the staff of the Almeida Theatre who not only provided an excellent venue, but were constant in their support throughout the project.

If you'd like further information on *Look, Europe!* please contact Joe Hipgrave at *Index*.

Roger Lloyd Pack – Credit: Carlos Reyes-Manzo/Andes

KAVEH GOLESTAN & NAHID RANJBAR

Privacy behind bars

THESE photographs were taken inside the women's ward of Tehran's infamous Evin prison, probably the most carefully guarded 'no-go' areas in the whole of Iran. They are the result of a four year project in the photographic studies section of Tehran's Arts University. The project aimed to break the taboo on photography in no-go areas such as prisons, mental asylums, drugs rehabilitation centres and so on. Implementing the project became a grotesque paperchase for permits, clearances and permissions: an exercise in official confrontation in the hope of creating tolerance among the toughest in the 'restriction business'.

The photographs were eventually shown alongside other prison photos – including a children's prison – in a public park in Tehran last year as part of a seminar dealing with social issues.

Since the victory of the Islamic Revolution in Iran, the country has been no friend to freedom of expression, nor, indeed, to any other freedom. In the cultural sphere, to paraphrase an old saying, 'this camel [of censorship] has slept behind everyone's gates': writers, film-makers, musicians, playwrights, painters, sculptors.

Though seldom happy, the human experience in Iran over the last 18 years has been rich and complex; there is still a lot to know – and understand – about Iran.

State censorship from within has been the main obstacle to the telling of this tale by those with the experience to know: the information vacuum has been all too readily exploited by those outside the country – exiles in the main plus commentators in the international media – happy to dish up a confection of error and misinformation to a gullible audience.

After 18 years, thanks to the efforts of those who remained inside the country and fought it, the vast edifice of censorship is shaking at its foundations. There were those who 'opposed', stood their ground, defied ideological intimidation; those who 'resisted' by working their way round the obstacles. Like the banned writer who secured his permit to print by passing off his new work as translations from an obscure writer of antiquity; the painter who continued to exhibit her banned work in a public art gallery – but wrapped in sackcloth and bound with rope; the sculptor who exhibited the unworked bark of a tree in the shape of a nude. Sparks that generated the energy to go on.

The women's section of Evin holds prisoners aged from 16 years old. The most common charges are prostitution, theft, murder and narcotics related crimes. Sentences range from a few months to life.

According to Asadollah Kajevardi, director of prisons:

- 58 per cent – 106,000 – of the country's prison population have been convicted on narcotics charges;
- HIV is present among these;
- 1.5 million health checks, including vaccinations, have been carried out on prisoners;
- more than 2,500 prisoners have learned the Quran by heart while doing time.

Although they have been part of this resistance, eye witnesses to life in revolutionary Iran, photographers had a particular problem: unlike artists of the imagination, they needed access, physical proximity to their subjects.

Today, a new generation of young Iranian photographers refuses to accept the taboos placed in the way of their work and the barriers are falling. What they want to show and tell of their life, their experience and their need to communicate it can no longer be contained – even behind the bars of Evin prison. ❏

*Photographs by **Nahid Ranjbar**, a graduate from the Arts University of Tehran. She works for various publications in Tehran.*
*Text by **Kaveh Golestan**, Iranian photo and video journalist living in Tehran. He was awarded the Robert Capa Prize for Photography for his coverage of the Revolution.*

BABEL

Talking about Jerusalem

MALU HALASA

THE search for a political solution to the problem of Jerusalem, claimed by both Jews and Arabs as their political and spiritual capital, has been at the centre of any Arab-Israeli negotiations since the Sykes-Picot agreement in 1916. Once the preserve of statesmen and diplomats, in recent years plans for the city's future have become the business of think tanks, symposiums and clandestine meetings – and not just in the Middle East.

Last spring, Palestinians and Israelis, including Likud politician Meir Shetreet, PLO representative Afif Safieh, Peace Now's lawyer Daniel Seidemann and Israeli academic Ruth Lapidoth, met secretly in Britain at the invitation of the UK Foreign and Commonwealth Office. According to independent observers, the Israelis were keen to press ahead and issue recommenda-tions. The Palestinians wanted the Israeli govern-ment to first acknowledge the dire situa-tion of the Arab inhabitants in East Jerusalem. The talks stalled before they began.

View from the ramparts of the old city – Credit: Malu Halasa

At another meeting, also joint and secret, three basic principals were formulated: Israelis would not allow the holy places – the Dome of the Rock, the Western Wall and the Church of the Holy Sepulchre – to be controlled by the Palestinians; local autonomy could be arranged for Arab East Jerusalem; and a government seat created for the Palestinian Authority outside city limits in the village of Abu Dis.

At both meetings no documents were signed, the world's press wasn't alerted. Months later, details from each meeting were leaked. The news of the second one made the main Palestinian negotiator, Abu Mazen, deny his involvement, even through his Israeli counterpart, Yossi Beilin, a Labour MP, discussed the plan at length in the Knesset.

Historically city plans have ignored the needs and opinions of Jerusalemites. Dividing the city or enlarging its boundaries have become political goals regardless of the very people whose lives they will most affect. During the 1948 war which established the Israeli State, Arab families either moved or fled to different sides of the city, and the barbed wire of the Green Line cut indiscriminately through Jewish and Palestinian homes and properties alike. After the Israeli victory in the 1967 Six Day War, Israeli families began to migrate eastward. Every time Jerusalem's political boundaries shift, new Jewish settlements are erected or new barriers set up, the result is upheaval and fear.

Bassem Eid heads a Palestinian human rights monitoring group, and lives in Shu'fat, Jerusalem's only refugee camp. His father, expelled from his land in Israel in 1948, came to Jerusalem for work and rented a house in the Jewish Quarter...

'WE still don't know why the Jordanian government moved us from the Jewish Quarter in 1966. They built a new refugee camp called Shu'fat. There were nine of us at that time and the house had two rooms three square metres each.

'I still live there. I'm married and have nine children. My seven brothers also live there and every one of us built two or three rooms and the house has three floors. We never talk about the plans for Jerusalem. The problem is when Yossi Beilin talks about the plan, Abu Mazen denies it. When Abu Mazen talks about the plan Yossi Beilin denies it and we don't know where the truth is.

'What I do know is that the house I left in 1966 costs US$1 million and the house I'm living in is worth US$10,000. The division of

Jerusalem is along economic lines first, although Palestinians have this idea that Muslims must keep the holy land. Nationalism also comes into it. Since it was the place of my birth I have the right to live here.'

Leila Dabdoub, an editor at Palestine/Israel Journal, *comes from an established, land-owning family who fled West Jerusalem in 1948, first to Ramallah, then Amman and Beirut before settling in East Jerusalem.*

'FOR me, to be honest, the property in West Jerusalem doesn't mean a thing because I didn't grow up there, but it means a lot to my family. When my grandmother was alive, she loved to go driving and see all the houses and shops she left behind. It's very painful to see your property inhabited by people to whom you have not rented or sold willingly. You go around like a stranger in your own home-town.

'It's by no means certain that the Israelis would offer Abu Dis as a seat for a Palestinian capital, but these are the rumours. I am not alone in reacting negatively. It is a big joke to give us something in a village which was in the district of Jerusalem but now is not because Abu Dis belongs to the district of Bethlehem according to the Israeli division. So East Jerusalemites scream and squirm but to no avail.'

General Uzi Narkiss commanded the Israeli troops who captured East Jerusalem during the 1967 Six Day War.

'LISTEN, I'm an old timer who did what he had to do. Now it is a different world. I was one of the combatants in the Palmach who fought in Jerusalem, but in 1948 we were too weak and the Arab legion was much stronger than us. So the end product resulted in a divided Jerusalem. It remains this way for 19 years. OK, all of a sudden comes 1967. We didn't have any other choice but to fight. Nobody planned to occupy the eastern part of Jerusalem. It was improvised only with the forces I managed to bring to battle, three brigades of about 2,000 people each. We had many casualties. At that time I was not the only one to be naive. Everybody thought that after such a brilliant victory the Arabs would settle for peace.

'Netanyahu said Peres would divide or redivide Jerusalem, which was not true but still it was successful as a campaign slogan. Personally I am against it totally and vehemently but I think we will need a compromise with the Palestinians, like the one we had in 1967 thanks to a smart man, Moshe Dayan, who returned Temple Mount to the Muslim authorities. From a realistic point of view, I am for a compromise. I am also counting on a backlash. People change their minds, other people come to power. I cannot allow myself to become desperate or defeatist. When the end comes, if it comes, you cannot imagine the profound despair.'

Sarah Kaminker, a Zionist, came to Israel from the US in 1967. A city planner under Mayor Teddy Kollek, she served for five years on the city council.

'THE mayor asked me to take charge of planning all the neighbourhoods in East Jerusalem and that was an eye opener. I saw the kind of plans that exist today: plans that prevent Arabs from using their land, plans that concentrate the Arab population in ever smaller pieces of property and confine the neighbourhoods to a small portion of the land they own. Since they cannot build housing, their housing conditions are really terrible.

'Jerusalem is a completely segregated city. The Jews who live in East Jerusalem were brought there for the purpose of changing the demographic balance in East Jerusalem, an extremely successful policy on the part of the municipality. Land was added to West Jerusalem for the purposes of maintaining that demographic balance: 72 per cent Jews, 28 per cent Arabs. As soon as people become frightened that there are too many Arabs in Jerusalem they start thinking about land for building more Jewish neighbourhoods.

'Would Jews who live in East Jerusalem, as I do, be willing in the interests of peace to accept a payment for damages and leave their houses? There is no question. I would do it tomorrow, but whether my neighbours would be willing is another matter.'

*Palestinian film director **Marwan Darweish** has lived on both sides of Jerusalem, west and east.*

'THE main difference for me was that in the west I didn't feel comfortable. There wasn't any hostility but it wasn't friendly either. The Jewish holidays used to be strange. Everybody was with their families and we were stuck in the flat. I found it easier to live on the east side of town, although there were also difficulties, like coming home late at night. You were almost guaranteed to be stopped by the army. If you took a taxi from West Jerusalem, it didn't want to go to East Jerusalem.

'I'm worried about putting more walls, more divisions, in the town. More borders will create further gaps between two communities. I think there should be more of an effort to create living and public spaces where people would naturally meet. Ideally I should be able to go to West or East Jerusalem and not be scared or worried. The authorities need to be more creative and go beyond this ethnic localism of areas and quarters.'

Dalia Jayes emigrated to Israel from London when she was 23. An orthodox Jew, she secured a doctorate in medicinal chemistry and pharmacology this year.

' I TRAVEL on the buses but I would be worried to take my two children and I won't go to the centre of town or to crowded shopping malls, obviously prime targets for terrorists. When I first got here, there was an attack in Mehane Yehuda in the market, and I remember saying the next morning, 'I can't go out today because it's dangerous.' My friends said, 'Well, you can't live like that.' After that I realised you have to carry on. Jerusalem is the undivided capital of the Jewish people. There is no other way.'

Yehuda Amichai, a poet, is from one of the few German families who emigrated to Israel in the early 1930s thus escaping the Holocaust.

' I have a poem that I just finished, right now. "Why not San Francisco? Why not London? There are other places that are much more beautiful. The question is, Why Jerusalem?" Should I use a very unpleasant metaphor? When you have a park and lots of wonderful trees and all the dogs go on one tree to do their things.

'Actually I've lived here from my early childhood and I went through everything. Of course I'm disappointed. We were 450,000 Jews in Palestine before World War II. Now we are 6 million and [after] so much immigrant waves, we the original settlers are dying out. It's like the first comers in any country, like the people from the Mayflower in America.

'I don't care about that, but I do think Zionism is the biggest revolution that mankind ever had. It was a revolution to get the Jewish people to speak their own language again and to be again a working people in their own land. After each revolution – alas, after the French and, alas, alas, after the Russian revolution – we see not exactly the 'counter revolution' but things mess up. You get either Napoleon or Stalin.

'Every year I say I'm going to leave Jerusalem. The problem is not only between Arabs and Jews but Arabs and Arabs and Jews and Jews. There is so much infighting. But still I live here. The most wonderful thing about Jerusalem is that I always find little corners that I don't know. It's the biggest small city in the world.' ❏

Malu Halasa is a freelance journalist living in London. She was in Jerusalem earlier this year

CHATHAM GRAMMAR SCHOOL
FOR GIRLS